CLASSIC CYC...

London & the South East

SURI
COUNTY CO

CLASSIC CYCLE CLIMBS

London & the South East

Adrian Bond

THE CROWOOD PRESS

First published in 2014 by
The Crowood Press Ltd
Ramsbury, Marlborough
Wiltshire SN8 2HR

www.crowood.com

British Library Cataloguing-in-Publication Data
A catalogue record for this book is available from the British
Library.

ISBN 978 1 84797 760 1

Typeset by Jean Cussons Typesetting, Diss, Norfolk
Printed and bound in India by Replika Press Pvt Ltd

CONTENTS

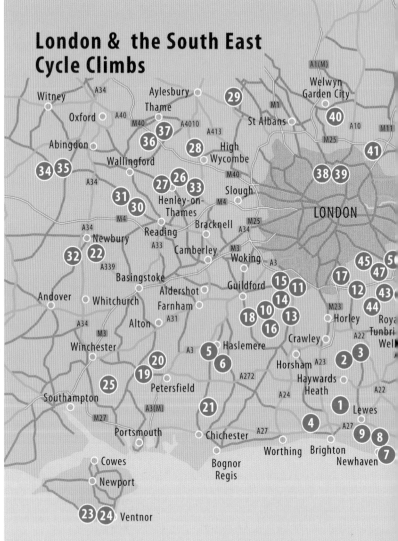

London & the South East Cycle Climbs

Witney
Oxford
Abingdon
Wallingford
Newbury
Basingstoke
Andover
Whitchurch
Alton
Winchester
Southampton
Portsmouth
Cowes
Newport
Ventnor

A34
A40
M40
A4010
A413
A34
A33
A339
A31
A34
M3
A3
M27
A3(M)
A27

Aylesbury
Thame
High Wycombe
St Albans
Slough
Henley-on-Thames
Reading
Bracknell
Camberley
Woking
Guildford
Aldershot
Farnham
Haslemere
Petersfield
Chichester
Bognor Regis
Worthing
Welwyn Garden City
LONDON
Horley
Crawley
Horsham
Haywards Heath
Lewes
Brighton
Newhaven
Royal Tunbridge Wells

A1(M)
M1
A10
M11
M25
M4
M25
A34
M3
M23
A22
A23
A24
A272
A27
A22

29
40
41
34 35
36 37
28
27 26 33
31 30
32 22
38 39
45 5
47
17
12 43
44
15 11
14
18 10 13
16
5 6
20
19
25
21
23 24

English Channel

↑N 20 km

ABOUT THE AUTHOR

Adrian Bond lives in South East London and is a cyclist first and foremost, and a writer some way after. He is yet to win an award in either discipline, although he did complete La Marmotte over the summer, a 174-kilometre sportive in the French Alps with 5,000 metres of climbing – probably the combined total of all the climbs featured in this book! He was bitten by the cycling bug aged 14, when he rode from Birmingham to Lands End, back in the days when he was contractually obliged to call his mother every evening from a public phone box. Now, of course, he uses his mobile.

ACKNOWLEDGEMENTS

Thanks to all the cyclists (and non-cyclists) I have met along the way who have shared their local knowledge and helped enormously in putting this all together, making this a guidebook 'by cyclists, for cyclists'. Particular thanks to Duncan for his input into the climbs of his native Berkshire (if he described a hill in overly vulgar terms it was generally worth checking out).

Special thanks must go to my riding companions and part-time models, Nic and Nick (aka the Nic & Nick Modelling Agency) for patiently riding up the same hill on repeat whilst I tried to get some arty shots. My lovely sister Sarah, and fab Rachael (plus Jade) for all of the above, plus inspiration and continued encouragement. Not forgetting Mike W, whom I cruelly dragged out to some of these hills.

Finally, thanks to Crowood Press for allowing me the opportunity to fulfil an ambition.

ABOUT THE BOOK

The book is divided by county, starting in Sussex then running in an anti-clockwise direction and finishing in Kent. The climbs are ordered alphabetically within each of the counties.

Each description starts with a table of facts about the climb, including a difficulty rating out of 10 within the context of the 50 climbs listed in the book. Also included is the address of a local café or tearoom where tired riders can compare their own experience over a tea or coffee and slice of cake.

Difficulty	○○○○○○○○○○
Distance	0.42km
Av. Gradient	10.7%
Max. Gradient	20%
Height Gain	45m
Start Point	At bridge (over Cob Brook), just off B2028
Local Cafés	Wakehurst Place Seed Café, Ardingly RH17 6TN ☎ 01444 894040

The map shows the start and finish point of the climb and the route it follows. We would recommend taking an OS map or a GPS system to help in plotting your route in more detail.

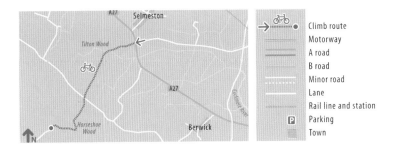

→🚲••••••• •	Climb route
	Motorway
	A road
	B road
	Minor road
	Lane
	Rail line and station
P	Parking
	Town

At the end of the book is a list of bike shops in the region, organized in book order. Each bike shop relates to one or more of the climbs so there'll be one nearby if you're in need of spares, repairs or just some good local advice.

INTRODUCTION

To cyclists, hills are like playgrounds. Mountains are more like theme parks. Going upwards is the ultimate test for us bike riders: it is the quickest way to gauge your fitness level, provides the best workout and eventually earns you the reward of an exhilarating descent. In the words of many a mountaineer, 'Because it's there' sums up what hills mean to cyclists. By researching this guide, I have ridden climbs I had only heard about. It has been very satisfying to tick some of these hills off the list. With the popularity of Strava, tackling these hills has the added appeal of pitting yourself against the rest of the cycling community, even the chance to compare your performance against the pros.

In this guide I have attempted to compile a guide to some of the best hills in the South East. It is not a Top 50 'best of' list – more a selection of some varied and interesting ascents covering geographical regions. Of course, some counties are more blessed with lumpy bits than others, so apologies to the likes of Hertfordshire, but it really is your fault for being mostly flat!

You may, naturally, have a different opinion on some of the hills; I may have overlooked one of your favourites (or is that least favourite?) but I hope, like me, you get the chance to ride some of these classic climbs. There should be something for everyone, so get out there and enjoy.

1. DITCHLING BEACON

Difficulty	⊘⊘⊘⊘⊘⊘⊘○○○
Distance	1.47km
Av. Gradient	9%
Max. Gradient	12%
Height Gain	135m
Start Point	At crossroads with Underhill Lane, south of village of Ditchling
Local Cafés	Ditchling Tea Rooms, 6–8 West Street, Hassocks, BN6 8TS ☎ 01273 842708

Anyone who has ridden the London to Brighton charity bike ride will know all about this unforgiving 'leg killer', coming as it does 80 kilometres into the route, as legs begin to get weary. Its constant gradient changes offer challenges at every turn.

As the highest point in East Sussex, it looms large – like a beacon, unsurprisingly. From the village of Ditchling approximately one and a half kilometres away (where you can fuel up at the tea rooms on West Street), the 'Green Monster', as it has been tagged, provides a picturesque backdrop. Approaching the climb along Beacon Road there is a slight uphill drag, with a clear view of what is to come.

The climb itself starts just as you reach the Underhill Lane crossroads; don't be tempted to turn off – just follow the road as it continues on and veers off to a sharp left (watch out for vehicles here, including cyclists descending at speed). The gradient

increases slightly but you can stay seated and get into a good rhythm; you should be able to stay in a mid-sprocket gear too for the first half a kilometre as you ride through a canopy of trees. The road surface is pretty good but there are some stray stones that need to be avoided.

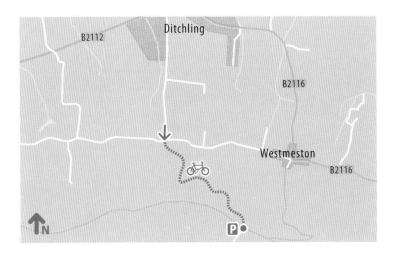

As the road turns to the right it also turns upwards but a few pedal strokes out of the saddle should get you over this short rise. In the shade of the wooded escarpment you can comfortably stay seated, but looking ahead you can see a couple of rollercoaster rises where again you may need to go to a lower gear and power over, with some flatter 'platforms' interspersed. At approximately one kilometre into the climb, the gradient really starts to bite. A sharp left-hander and the view opens out wonderfully to the left. Don't be fooled into thinking this is the top though, as it is not over yet. Back into the trees again and the short ramps continue to disrupt the tempo.

Around a dragging left bend, grinding out of the saddle, and you are out of the woods (literally). The view of the downs on a clear day is fantastic, but you can enjoy that fully at the top. Once you see the signpost warning of horses, there is just a tough 80 metre ramp up to the summit and a nice clear area to pull into on the left to recuperate and enjoy the vista.

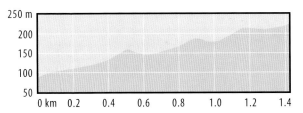

THE GREEN MONSTER

Ditchling Beacon was featured in the Tour de France back in 1994, when the biggest cycle race in the world made one of its regular visits to the UK. Sean Yates (who lived locally) was one of the few British riders back then who rode in Le Tour. He told of tackling this climb on a gear of 42 × 16. For most of us mere mortals, at least a lowest gear of 39 × 21 would be needed. During the charity bike ride every June, the climb causes what can only be described as devastation, with hundreds of less experienced cyclists either crawling their way up or forced to walk their bikes up the one and a half kilometres, before enjoying the glorious freewheel descent into Brighton.

Being the highest point in Sussex, the beacon was the site of an Iron Age fort. According to a local resident, in the days of the horse and cart it was possible to hire a cock horse at the base of the hill, to assist with successfully hauling a cart to the top of the beacon. On the climb itself, you may notice the short flattened sections – a feature of the time when horses were given a chance to rest on their difficult journey without the cart rolling back.

Today, the climb has become notorious as a 'must do' for every keen cyclist. In my opinion it does have something of an aura about it, particularly as it seems to attract a regular pilgrimage of cyclists to ride up the 'Green Monster'. If you haven't tried it yet, have a go and see if you can get anywhere near the fastest time of 4 minutes 19 seconds!

2. COB LANE

Difficulty	◉ ◉ ◉ ◉ ◉ ◉ ◉ ◉ ○ ○
Distance	0.42km
Av. Gradient	10.7%
Max. Gradient	20%
Height Gain	45m
Start Point	At bridge (over Cob Brook), just off B2028
Local Cafés	Wakehurst Place Seed Café, Ardingly RH17 6TN ☎ 01444 894040

The wooded climb up Cob Lane in West Sussex is a sweeping brute hitting gradients of 20%, sandwiched in the High Wealds between the North and South Downs. It is located on the outskirts of the village of Ardingly (Cob Lane is hidden away just off the B2028). The London to Brighton bike ride passes by en route to Ditchling Beacon (which is only thirty minutes' ride from here), so this could be a good warm up!

The ascent begins just after you cross the narrow bridge (beware of approach-

ing cars) over Cob Brook and with woodland all around you, the road is single track so keep an eye on your line on some of the blind bends. Within 50 metres you are scrambling for the lowest gear (27- or 28-tooth sprocket would be recommended) and it's out of the saddle as your speed drops dramatically. The first 150 metres has you fighting to turn the pedals as it suddenly

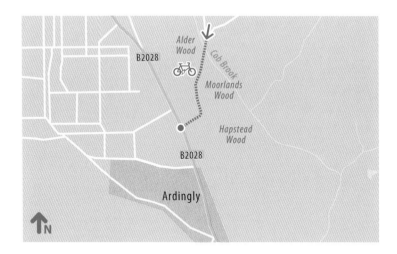

and rudely approaches the 20% mark through snaking S-bends. Depending on the time of year you may find a coating of leaves on the surface which could cause some slipping. As the road curves to the left there's a chance to get back in the saddle for a precious few metres' recovery but it is quite short-lived. Here the woodland to your left opens up a little to offer glimpses of the surrounding rolling hills. As the road then veers sharply to the right, it again steepens and another burst out of the saddle may well be in order and with it the burn starts all over again. It may be short but it is a long way from sweet!

Keep fighting onwards and upwards, it will soon be over as its just 50 short but painful metres up to the B2028, and the village of Ardingly (birthplace of newscaster and keen cyclist Jon Snow).

Turning right will take you past the South of England Showground to Wakehurst Place (Kew's lesser known country garden) which has a great café with sun terrace, serving a fine selection of cakes, sausage rolls and toasties.

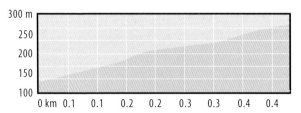

3. KIDDS HILL

Difficulty	◉ ◉ ◉ ◉ ◉ ◉ ◉ ◉ ○ ○
Distance	1.57km
Av. Gradient	7.9%
Max. Gradient	12%
Height Gain	124m
Start Point	Just over small bridge in hamlet of Newbridge
Local Cafés	Riverview Café, Station Road, Forest Row RHI8 5DW ☎ 01342 823030

Deep in the majestic Ashdown Forest in Sussex (the setting for AA Milne's *Winnie the Pooh*), Kidds Hill is not to be taken in jest, as its nickname 'The Wall' accurately suggests. Those who have ridden The Hell of the Ashdown or The King of the Downs sportives will be very familiar with this daunting climb.

The wooded ascent starts as you cross over the stone walled bridge (caution: oncoming traffic has priority here) near the settlement of Newbridge (which is about 4 kilometres southeast of Forest Row) and for the first hundred metres it is relatively gentle, so you can get into something of a rhythm. The gradient quickly steepens though and with a high bank to your left hand

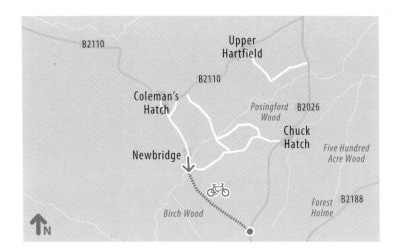

side, it is out of the saddle and down to your biggest sprocket as it hits an incline of around 12%. As the road veers to the left it eases for another 100 metres but then it's another short, steep rise to test the legs. 80 metres later the road meanders right to left and as you pass Cobbers Farm, the hardest part of the climb reveals itself and you are looking pretty much straight down the barrel to the summit. The tunnel of trees continues all the way and the light at the end is very clear to see. By this point it will certainly be starting to hurt.

As the lactic acid builds, you must keep turning the gear over and keep positive as it's a steady but tough 10% gradient to the clearing. As you pass the canopy of the forest, the worst is over and with views of the gorse-covered moors it is a much easier gradient.

Despite the burning legs and lungs, you can drop down a couple of gears, get your breath back and drag yourself over the last 200 gentler, rolling metres to the main road – the B2026.

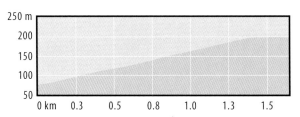

4. STEYNING BOSTAL

Difficulty	⊙⊙⊙⊙⊙⊙⊙○○○
Distance	2.02km
Av. Gradient	7.1%
Max. Gradient	17%
Height Gain	119m
Start Point	Junction with Clays Hill/Bramber Road and Bostal Road
Local Cafés	Café 33, 33 Warwick Street, Worthing BN11 3DQ ☎ 01903 200080

This climb out of the town of Steyning in West Sussex is used by Brighton Mitre Cycling Club for their annual hill climb competition in October. It looks innocuous at first, starting in a leafy residential area, but twists and turns later up a brutal gradient through a chalk valley. Eventually summiting at the top of a picturesque ridge, there are fantastic sweeping views down to the coast (on a clear day).

Starting from the left, turn off Clays Hill/Bramber Road at the southern end of the town, and onto Bostal Road; you pass the single track road sign, and the gradual

ascent bisects houses to either side of you. Then, as you enter the cover of trees after approximately 200 metres the gradient starts to increase. The road sweeps to the left and then right and it is out of the saddle for the next 150 metres or so as the gradient hits 13% in places, before it levels off significantly

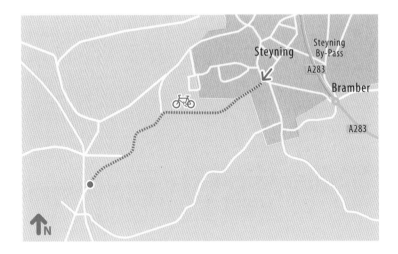

for a small respite of around 300 metres and you can drop down a couple of gears and catch your breath for the next, more challenging section.

As the road veers sharply to the left (be aware of vehicles turning onto the road from the right), it really ramps up now and it is onto the largest sprocket quick smart, for a section that maxes out at 17–18%. The road really opens up here with a chalk escarpment to your right and a great view over rolling fields towards the sea on your near side. Standing on the pedals you are really working hard now to keep your momentum.

Another bend to the left, and a small respite of 50 metres of lesser gradient, before one final surge over the 80 metres to the summit, where there is a chance to stop and appreciate the well-earned vista.

The road continues atop of the ridge before plummeting down to the sea towards Worthing (although you do have to cross the busy A27 dual carriageway with care).

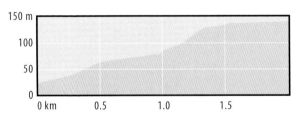

5. TENNYSON'S LANE

Difficulty	◉◉◉◉◉○○○○○
Distance	2.08km
Av. Gradient	3.9%
Max. Gradient	15%
Height Gain	80m
Start Point	Junction of Petworth Road and Haste Hill
Local Cafés	Darnleys Coffee Shop, 3 High Street, Haslemere GU27 2JZ ☎ 01428 643048

This lane is named after the famous poet who lived locally and who described Blackdown thus: 'You came and looked and loved the view, long known and loved by me, Green Sussex fading into blue with one grey glimpse of sea'. Unfortunately he didn't write about cycling up this climb to Blackdown via Tennyson's Lane. It can be climbed from both directions but for ease of locating, the climb to the top of Blackdown (the highest point in Sussex) is described from the Haslemere side.

From town take the B2131 (named Petworth Road) and after 300 metres turn right onto Haste Hill. It starts with a bang so hastily go for the gears and prepare to get out of the saddle almost immediately for 400 metres of struggle up an unrelenting ascent. As the road curves to the left it flattens out and you reach a crossroads. With caution, head straight on (signposted Tennyson's Lane Blackdown) to the single track road.

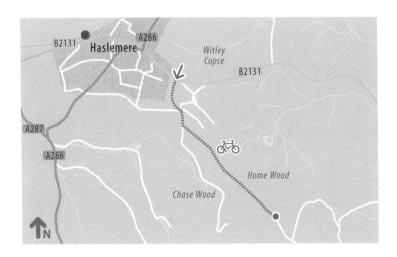

After about 100 metres riding through the wooded canopy, follow the road sharply to the left and stay on Tennysons Lane. For the next kilometre it plateaus at a very easy 1–2% as you pass through a residential area. You then hit woodland again and the road snakes upwards with a slight gradient increase but nothing too demanding, so you can stay comfortably seated as you meander through the pine trees, with an occasional glimpse of rolling hills. It really is a fantastic road now the hard gradient is behind you, with shafts of light cutting through the foliage.

The last 50 metres does rise up a bit (as you pass the car park to the right) and the National Trust sign for Blackdown signifies the unofficial summit at an elevation of 252 metres. If you carry on to the descent, be ready for a very tight left-hand bend in the first 300 metres (it can easily catch you out!).

Coming up from the other side there is a more consistent gradient and without the vertical challenge of Haste Hill. Turn off Fernden Lane for a lovely undulating 2 kilometres before you start climbing through the trees.

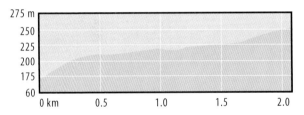

6. FERNDEN LANE

Difficulty	◉◉◉◉◉◉○○○○
Distance	1.04km
Av. Gradient	8.6%
Max. Gradient	19%
Height Gain	91m
Start Point	Junction of Jobsons Lane and Quell Lane (leads onto Fernden Lane)
Local Cafés	Darnleys Coffee Shop, 3 High Street, Haslemere GU27 2JZ ☎ 01428 643048

A very close neighbour to Tennyson's Lane in the South Downs National Park, near Haslemere, you can combine this ascent with the previously described Tennyson's Lane very easily if you are happy to have just a five-minute recovery in between! This great ascent (rising 91 metres in just over a kilometre) takes you along a rollercoaster single track road, and eventually loops you back in the direction of Haslemere.

Turning off Jobsons Lane onto Quell Lane, the first 400 metres undulates gently through delightfully tranquil woodland, the road dipping and rising in front of you. Everything in the world seems right but just as you are starting to lose yourself in a dream, the road bends to the left and incredibly rudely rises up to the skies. The gradient nears 20% on the curve and only marginally decreases over the next brutal

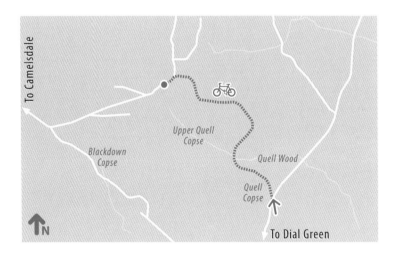

100 metres. There is also quite a lot of loose gravel so beware of wheels slipping here. It really is a case of putting your head down and fighting your way up. A 27- or 28-tooth sprocket would be recommended for the average cyclist; keeping the gear turning whilst seated might be necessary with the loose gravel and also if there are damp leaves on the road surface.

As you pass the driveway on the left, there are a few seconds of a flatter section, but this is not enjoyed for long and very soon you are back out of the saddle again for another ramp. The road narrows and bends to the right and there is no let-up for the legs. With a very grandiose house on your right-hand side, continue following the road to your left (marked Fernden Lane) and within 50 metres you are approaching the top, marked by an ancient mileage marker notifying 3¾ miles back to the town of Haslemere.

This great cycling road continues onwards for a further 5 kilometres or so (mostly downhill) and to the A286 which will lead you to Haslemere.

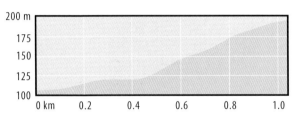

7. HIGH AND OVER

Difficulty	⊙⊙⊙⊙⊙⊙⊙○○○
Distance	1.06km
Av. Gradient	7.7%
Max. Gradient	15%
Height Gain	82m
Start Point	Adjacent to Frog Firle Farm on White Way/ Alfriston Road
Local Cafés	The Singing Kettle, Waterloo Square, Alfriston, Polegate BN26 5UD ☎ 01323 870723

This climb, on the Alfriston Road, heading towards the seaside town of Seaford (about 4 kilometres away) in East Sussex is a difficult customer. Its ever-changing gradient makes it hard to find any kind of rhythm and with a long continuous ramp at the end can really test the climbing legs. It does offer some great scenery, though, and the views at the top should hopefully make the effort all worthwhile.

Our starting point is just alongside Frog Firle Farm, in the slight dip after a fast, sweeping descent along White Way, heading towards Seaford.

As you leave the farm behind, the climb to High and Over begins with a sharp left-hander. With luck you should have some momentum from the downhill section of White Way to carry you over the first few metres; however, before you know it

you are hitting the low gears as you ride through a steep S-bend. As the road veers tightly to the right, the gradient hits 15% but it's a short, sharp ramp and then the road levels to a much more manageable 3%. Make the most of this relief, for the road takes a long, gradual turn to the left and you are back in the big sprocket for a long drawn-out section where it hits 9%.

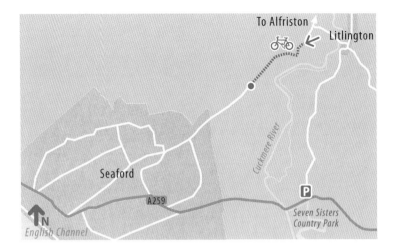

The views of the rolling hills offer some distraction, but keep the gazing to a minimum as the road can get busy at times. The gradient continues at this energy-sapping level for about the next 200 metres, before it eases for an all-too-brief moment. At roughly the halfway point it is out of the saddle as tiring legs start to falter and the gradient increases up to 13%. It is now a case of hanging on for the last 250 metres, as there is little let-up.

Passing the sign for the car park (signifying 180 yards) where this climb finishes, gives some encouragement. Keep pushing on over the top and roll into the car park, where (if you are lucky enough to get a clear day) you'll get a great view down to the coast. The nearest café is 2 kilometres away in the picture postcard village of Alfriston. Descending back down High and Over is fast and beware the sharp left hander near the bottom. Alternatively, continue on down to Seaford for a wider choice of eateries and a bike shop (Mr Cycles).

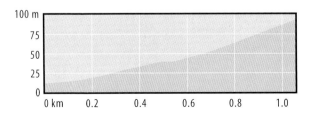

8. BO-PEEP LANE

Difficulty	◎◎◎◎◎◎◎○○○
Distance	2.37km
Av. Gradient	5.4%
Max. Gradient	25%
Height Gain	128m
Start Point	At crossroads with Common Lane off A27
Local Cafés	Firle Place, Firle, Lewes BN8 6LP ☎ 01273 858307

This wonderfully quiet and scenic ascent in the South Downs of East Sussex provides a contrasting mix of emotions. The rolling first kilometre through peaceful woodland opens out to some fantastic views and it is some of the best cycling you could experience, but the tough climax to the ascent could potentially sour things somewhat. Upon reaching the top, you have the reward of a stunning vista.

To start there is over a kilometre of gentle meandering lane through woodland to enjoy, and ample time to get the legs warmed up. The climbing doesn't start until you reach Bo-Peep Farmhouse Bed and Breakfast on your left-hand side. Entering into

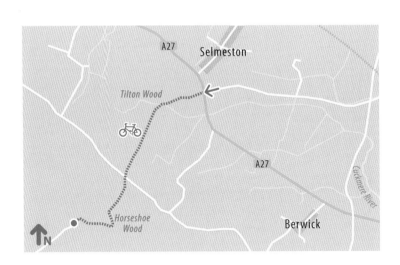

a tunnel of trees, with just birdsong (and heavy breathing) to accompany you, the gradient rises to 5%. It then increases quickly and though you can stay seated, you are dropping down the gears. Coming out of the cover of the trees briefly, the road bends to the left, the gradient touching 12%. It eases slightly over the next 100 metres as you head back into the woods again before the road turns sharply to the right and suddenly you are fighting over a 1 in 4 ramp. The natural instinct is to stand on the pedals; however, with a greasy road surface here it may be prudent to keep some weight on the back tyre (not necessarily easy).

Around the switchback and with high, grassy banks on either side the battle is not won yet. It is a case of staying strong and carrying on pedalling, as the gradient barely drops below 12% from here on in. After 200 metres the road sweeps to the left and the hill has another attempt to break you on another steep, steep ramp. Pushing over this last 80 metre hurdle the summit is waiting. Whimper into the car park and once your head has stopped spinning, enjoy the view.

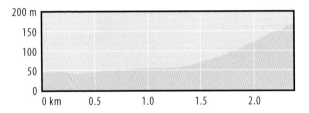

9. FIRLE BOSTAL

Difficulty	⊙⊙⊙⊙⊙⊙⊙⊙◯◯
Distance	1.95km
Av. Gradient	7.2%
Max. Gradient	14%
Height Gain	141m
Start Point	In village of West Firle, take Firle Bostal road from beside school
Local Cafés	Little Cottage Tea Rooms, Ranscombe Lane, Glynde BN8 6ST ☎ 01273 858215

Situated just a few kilometres from the previously described Bo-Peep Lane climb, you can easily combine the two, depending on remaining energy levels. Again this ascent leads off from the main A27 (approximately 6 kilometres from the town of Lewes) and is basically just a lane up to a car park for the South Downs Way walk, so once away from the A27 it is a fantastically peaceful haven.

The climb starts about 400 metres away from the main road at the village of West Firle. By the school, take the turn marked Firle Bostal. It is quite narrow here so do beware of any traffic. The first 700 metres or so is a gentle, gentle gradient followed by a short downhill (how generous) before the road opens up to reveal a fantastic view up to the beacon. Passing the terraced cottages on the left, the proper climbing starts.

The road continues straight ahead and you can see on the incline of the road what appear to be almost mini-terraces in the gradient. Suffice to say they don't help a great deal. Quickly you are out of the saddle for this first section. Going around a chicane the gradient travels to 12%

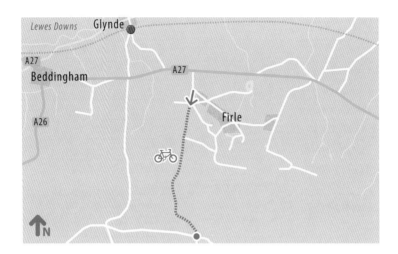

and once you've negotiated this it eases for a while to less than 5%. But as is so often the case it is not long before you are back out of the saddle, approaching the chalky outcrop. Up ahead you can now see the long and winding road as it wraps around the escarpment.

A short ramp to get over and with the land dropping away to your left, there is a short respite as the road curves around to the left. The steeper section now comes into view and soon you are pushing up the 300 metre stretch with a gradient varying between 11% and 14% and it seems to last forever. It is also quite exposed so the elements could make this section even more difficult; however, you can be momentarily distracted from the pain by the amazing scenery.

Heaving to the top, you reach the entrance to the car park and an elevation of 166m where you can really take in the views. Descend back to the main road and turn off to the village of Glynde for some great service at the Little Cottage Tea Rooms, Ranscombe Lane.

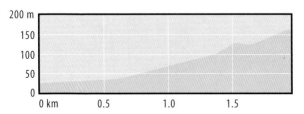

10. WALKING BOTTOM

Difficulty	◉◉◉◉◯◯◯◯◯◯
Distance	2.1km
Av. Gradient	6.2%
Max. Gradient	12%
Height Gain	104m
Start Point	Outside Hurtwood Inn and Pedal & Spoke bike shop in village of Peaslake
Local Cafés	Peaslake village store, Peaslake Lane, Guildford GU5 9RL ☎ 01306 730474

From the picturesque and quaint village of Peaslake in the Surrey Hills, the climb along Walking Bottom could be described by many as barely a hill. It's certainly not a thigh-burning wall but it is memorable for just being a really enjoyable cycling experience, a

gentle S-bend ascent (albeit with a couple of lumpy bits) through peaceful woodland (popular with the mountain biking community). It is a great little road!

As you leave Peaslake, starting at the inviting Hurtwood Inn and the last of the village houses, it eases along for roughly 400 metres (with a short false flat) before the road veers left for the first of two short, sharp shocks. It's up and out of the saddle for 80 metres and into the lowest gears, as the gradient increases to 8% and then 12%; be mindful of your line here as there are a few chunky potholes. Continue past a right-hand turn (Lawbrook Lane), follow the road straight on

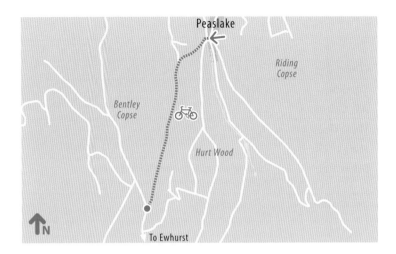

and the gradient eases somewhat before another hard rise, where you may need to stand on the pedals to push over.

With the couple of leg burning ramps out of the way it then settles into a consistent 5% gradient for the rest of the way up. The road winding gently through a fern lined wood, it is a cracking little stretch with hardly any traffic and you can push a mid-sprocket gear and get a good tempo going, enjoying one of the quieter lanes in the Surrey Hills, far from the madding crowds at Box Hill. It would be a perfect climb for interval training and you can push as hard as your heart desires over this final section.

The climb continues on to the junction with Hound House Road (where this climb ends). If you want to get a few more metres of elevation, turning right will take you to the crest of the summit and the turn off to Barhatch Road which in turn will lead you down to Barhatch Lane (if you really want to test your climbing legs).

Heading back into Peaslake you can get a tea and hot snack at the village store (you can't miss it).

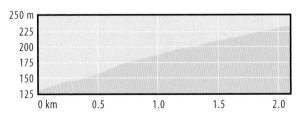

11. BOX HILL

Difficulty	◉◉◉◉◉○○○○○
Distance	2.42km
Av. Gradient	5.2%
Max. Gradient	16%
Height Gain	126m
Start Point	Turning from Old London Road onto Zig Zag Road
Local Cafés	Café at summit

This climb in the Surrey Hills has become notorious in recent years as a mecca for cyclists, almost the South East's Alpe d'Huez (but with about 80% fewer switchbacks and 90% less difficulty). With the Olympic road race tackling it nine times it became

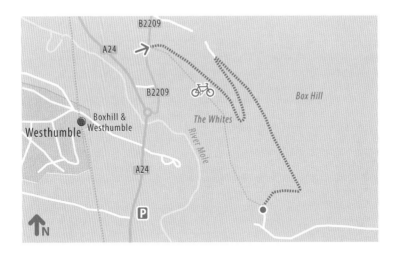

even more famous and one of the 'go to' climbs for local cyclists. Over 17,000 cyclists have recorded times for this famous climb on Strava, the quickest being an incredible 4 minutes 43 seconds (5 minutes 51 seconds for the ladies) – so something to aim for! At an average of around 5% it is really not that difficult, and it is ideal for interval training sessions (you'll often see cyclists doing it on repeat).

Turning off the B2209 onto the single lane road (beware of cars and oncoming cyclists as you turn), the first kilometre gently weaves through the lower woodland. Starting at 4% it slightly increases to 6% and a good tempo can be achieved in a middle sprocket. As you pass a small car park on the left, you soon hit a hairpin that bends to the left. The view opens up with a vast grassy escarpment on your right. The easy gradient continues as you go over the occasional speed bump and head back beneath the cover of trees before you sharply turn right on the second hairpin and encounter a short ramp in the gradient (keep tucked into the left as cars and cyclists descend in the centre of the road).

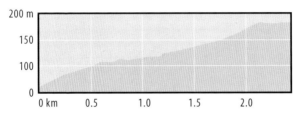

The road then straightens out and you can enjoy a great view to your right, and get inspired by the names of Wiggins and Froome still painted on the road. With the gradient sticking at around 5%, it's fairly comfortable to keep a strong tempo. Going back under the canopy of trees there is a sharp bend to the right, where the road narrows. After a slight bend to the left and car parks on both sides of the road, the summit is fast approaching; here lies an opportunity to have refreshments at the café and, moving a little further up the road, a fantastic view.

TOP OF THE BOX

Box Hill is one of the most popular segments on Strava; over 16,000 cyclists have registered 73,000 (and counting) attempts on this climb. Many of these were posted during the inaugural Ride London event in August 2013 when 20,000 amateur cyclists tackled Box Hill on the Olympic road race course. The Olympic race famously went over Box Hill nine times of course, the organisers of Ride London being far more sympathetic. Later on the same day, the professionals followed suit, which explains the number of pro riders at the top of the leader board. Currently the King of the Mountain leading time for the segment is 4 minutes 47 seconds, which translates to an impressive average speed of 18 mph.

In comparison, my personal attempts on Strava have been somewhat disappointing. The method of 'ride 200 metres and stop to write notes for a guidebook' is not conducive to impressive times.

12. CHALKPIT LANE

Difficulty	⦿ ⦿ ⦿ ⦿ ⦿ ⦿ ⦿ ⦿ ○
Distance	1.89km
Av. Gradient	7.8%
Max. Gradient	20%
Height Gain	148m
Start Point	Junction with Barrow Green Road
Local Cafés	Café Papillon, 54 Station Road West, Oxted RH8 9EU ☎ 01883 717031

The mere mention of Chalkpit Lane can make even the most hardened of cyclists go weak at the knees. It's a killer, frankly, and not to be attempted with tired legs! It goes over the same escarpment as Titsey, but 2 kilometres further west and seemingly straight up and over rather than easing the rider into a gentler route!

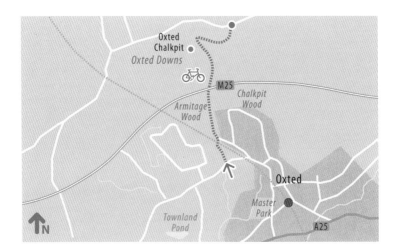

For ease of description the climb starts at the junction with Barrow Green Road, about a kilometre and a half north of the town of Oxted. For the first kilometre there is a chance to get your legs warmed up on the very gentle incline through a residential area with a great view of the mass of chalk rockface ahead. Then the road continues at a steady 4% gradient as you pass under the railway bridge. You approach the underpass of the M25 and you can feel the gradient starting to increase as it nears 7%; looking across to your right at the steeply angled field, you get an idea of what's to come!

The road then narrows to a single lane and it is soon time to test the strength of your legs (and your mind). For the next 200 metres the gradient rises to 9% as you pass the Oxted quarry on the left and into the shade of the trees.

Passing the sign warning of gradients of 20%, the reality hits and suddenly the road sweeps steeply to the right. The urge to get out of the saddle is immense but with the thick canopy of trees there is a real danger of the road being slippery, even in summer, so be wary of losing rear wheel grip. Pushing a gear of 34 × 27 you can keep

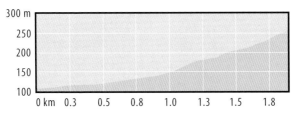

seated (just) and get through this 20% rise but then there is little let up for the next leg-bursting 200 metres. The urge to stop and lie down is overwhelming, but keep positive as the pain will soon end!

Going round a slight left-hander, you pass a solitary telegraph pole on the right where finally the vicious ramp starts to subside and you can manage a higher cadence and a lower heart rate as you mercifully hang on to reach the top and the junction with the Ridge.

13. LEITH HILL

Difficulty	⊙⊙⊙⊙⊙⊙⊙○○○
Distance	1.96km
Av. Gradient	6.9%
Max. Gradient	13%
Height Gain	136m
Start Point	At junction with B2126 (Ockley Road)
Local Cafés	Jampot Café, 6 Ranmore Road, Dorking RH4 1HA ☎ 01306 875591

This climb, as the thousands of participants in the inaugural Ride London event will no doubt testify, is a much sterner test than its neighbour Box Hill, climbing 136m through woodland to an elevation of 250 metres. Situated to the southwest of Dorking, in the Surrey Hills, it is less than a kilometre from Forest Green.

Turning off the B2126 (Ockley Road) onto Leith Hill Lane (there is no road name but it is signposted 'Etherley Farm', for the campsite) the road undulates gently along through the cover of trees for the first 600 metres at around 3–4% and you can maintain a good speed. You then approach a narrowing of the road and the gradient climbs to 8% for a small section. The road surface is quite poor in some places along this section, so watch for potholes.

It then rises again up a short ramp as you pass the red brick wall on the right, flattening slightly with Leith Hill Place on

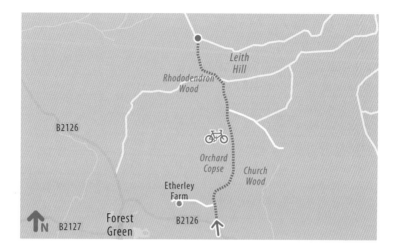

the left (a seventeenth-century gabled house now owned by the National Trust). A very short respite and the road then steepens; combined with a heavy road surface, it feels particularly hard for the next 100 metres. Making a sharp left (with Coldharbour turning off to the right), and then passing Tanhurst Lane one and a half kilometres in, it feels like you have made it to the finish line. But there is a sting in the tail. Keep following the road straight on and the gradient sharpens to 11% and then touches 13% as you grind over this difficult last ramp.

The last 300 metres feels like it is never going to end as you keep pushing on with heavy legs to quite an anti-climactic finish at the summit, with just a rather uninspiring car park on the left to pull into and rest. Neither is there a great view to enjoy, apart from woodland.

Afterwards, back track slightly and turn onto Abinger Road, which in turn will lead you to Coldharbour Lane (with a tad more climbing) en route to Dorking for refuelling.

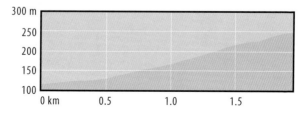

14. WHITEDOWN

Difficulty	⊙⊙⊙⊙⊙⊙⊙○○○
Distance	1.95km
Av. Gradient	6.5%
Max. Gradient	20%
Height Gain	128m
Start Point	At turnoff from A25
Local Cafés	R & P Sandwich and Coffee Bar, 242 High Street, Dorking RH4 1QR ☎ 01306 882929

If your legs are still feeling strong after tackling Leith Hill, you can ride on a further 4 kilometres in a northwesterly direction, and you can have a crack at this tough little climb in the Surrey Hills. It begins as you turn north off the A25 onto Whitedown Lane, approximately a kilometre from the quaint village of Sutton Abinger and 2 kilometres east of Gomshall, where you can find the nearest train station. It is a single lane road, so be wary of other traffic, particularly on the hairpins – including cyclists descending at speed. Also be careful of stones on the road surface.

Following the gradual lower slopes for a kilometre of gentle gradient (with a short drop at one point), it is not really until you pass over the railway bridge that the climb

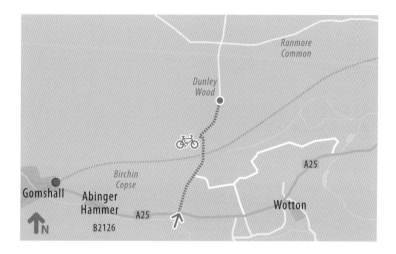

starts in earnest. Again it's the traditional English climb through woodland, and the first 70 metres gradually rises at 3% or so before the road turns sharply left and sharply upwards. It's into the big sprockets (a gear of 34 × 27 recommended) and very likely out of the saddle too as you push round, before the road hairpins to the right and you are suddenly pushing hard over a tough 20% ramp.

The road begins to straighten up, and the gradient eases ever so slightly to around 12–13%, but remains at this for just a bit too long! Passing a derelict stone building on your left, it feels as though your climbing legs have also been abandoned. Looking up towards the summit, shafts of sunlight seem to reflect off the chalky soil giving a strange ethereal hue to the climb (either that or I was suffering more than I thought).

Finally, in the last 200 metres the gradient begins to drop below 10% and after a final push it's an understated finish to the summit, as suddenly you start on the descent. If you continue straight on for 500 metres you can turn right onto Ranmore Common and head back towards Dorking for some well-deserved refreshment.

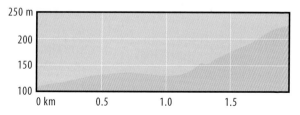

15. RANMORE COMMON

Difficulty	⭕⭕⭕⭕⭕⭕⭕⭕⭕⭕
Distance	1.69km
Av. Gradient	6.4%
Max. Gradient	17%
Height Gain	109m
Start Point	Junction with Chapel Road and Ranmore Common
Local Cafés	Café at Pilgrim Cycles, The Old Booking Hall, Boxhill and Westhumble Station, Surrey RH5 6BT ☎ 01306 886958

This very close relation to Box Hill in the Surrey Hills (being just 1.5 kilometres away from its better known and more popular sibling) is a gradual and slow burning climb, much quieter but providing a greater workout, in my opinion. It seems placid enough but push too hard early on and the ever-increasing gradient might find you out as you near the top.

It is relatively easy to find from Box Hill: turn onto Old London Road towards the A24. Turn left and almost immediately cross over the dual carriageway, following signs for Boxhill and Westhumble Station (next to which is a bike shop/café). This will take you onto Chapel Road.

After around 1.5 kilometres, turn left off Chapel Road onto Ranmore Common. It is a single-track road (some potholes and loose gravel on lower section) with a gentle 4% gradient for the first kilometre. You can maintain a good tempo in a mid-range gear for this first section.

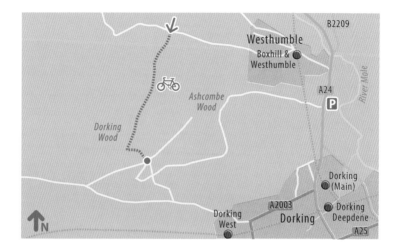

Passing the farmhouse on the right you can see the road gently snaking through the trees and still it looks innocuous enough. The road then sweeps to the left into dense woodland and gradually the incline rises with sections of 10%, and with every passing minute you are shifting to lower gears. If you are starting to feel it here the next section will come as a nasty surprise – the road hairpins sharply to the left and the camber is a vicious 17% as you crest the bend. It's a fight to keep the pedals turning but then it is back to a much kinder 5%.

Coming through the canopy of trees, and with a very green pond to your right the road rises to 8% but you can crest the summit as the road passes Denbigh House, veers to the right and flattens out.

This is a great hill for interval training, or if you just want to enjoy a great cycling road. Head back to Pilgrim Cycles at Boxhill and Westhumble Station for refreshments.

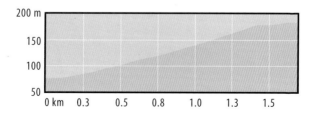

16. BARHATCH LANE

Difficulty	⊘ ⊘ ⊘ ⊘ ⊘ ⊘ ⊘ ⊘ ○
Distance	2.48km
Av. Gradient	6.7%
Max. Gradient	21%
Height Gain	165m
Start Point	At junction with Amlets Lane
Local Cafés	Cromwell Coffee House, 97 High Street, Cranleigh, GU6 8AU ☎ 01483 273783

Featured in the 2013 Tour of Britain (as a category 1 climb), this difficult ascent takes you deep into Winterfold/Hurtwood Forest, gaining a whopping 165 metres of eleva-

tion over almost 2.5 kilometres. It is situated just over a kilometre outside (supposedly) the largest village in the UK – Cranleigh. From there follow the B2127 northwest and turn off onto Barhatch Road.

The climb begins at the junction with Amlets Lane just by the quite worrying 21% warning sign, where Barhatch Road becomes Barhatch Lane. The first section, however, eases gently along with houses on your right and a gentle gradient of 4–7%, and it continues like this for the first kilometre. Then there is a short downhill section before you start climbing

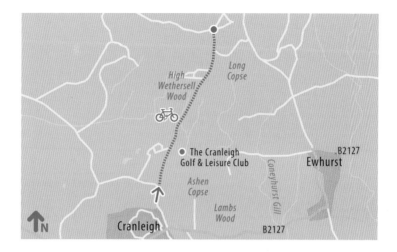

again, from a modest 4% quickly rising to 12% for a short period. By the time you reach the sign for Winterfold Farm, the climbing eases, albeit only for 80 metres. Then, approaching the next part of the climb, be prepared for the lowest gear you have, if you have a triple chainset with a 'granny ring' then I'm sure most cyclists would forgive you; failing that, a 34 × 28 would get the average rider up.

Back out of the saddle as you pass the red brick wall and farmhouse on your right, around a small left-hander and the road bottlenecks into a narrow and very steep section. The next 80 metres is, frankly, a wall, topping out at 21%, and it becomes a fight to keep the bike moving. As you pass the appropriately named Hurtwood House there is a tiny easing of gradient before the final metres to the summit and the turn off Greensand Lane. There is a car park you can quickly roll into here to compose yourself.

For fantastic home baked sausage rolls (and cake), drop back into Cranleigh and make for the Cromwell Coffee House.

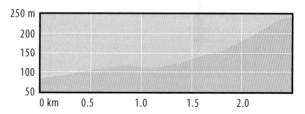

MAKING A MOLEHILL OUT OF A MOUNTAIN

The Tour of Britain cycle race is a regular visitor to Barhatch Lane, and the 2013 edition pulled in big crowds on this narrow and steep climb, eager for a glimpse of Sir Bradley, Cavendish and a quality field of riders including feather-light Colombian climber Nairo Quintana (he surely would fly up this 'little climb')?

With the road closed to vehicles about an hour before the race was due to pass by, hundreds of amateurs seized the opportunity to try their legs on the climb. Watching from the sidelines, it was reassuring to see that I was not the only one who struggled on this cruel 21% ascent. (In my defence I was on the heavier touring bike, with two full water bottles ... and I was wearing quite a chunky watch.) It was heart-warming to witness so many youngsters riding up too (they probably didn't need to make it look so easy though), and the future of this great sport looks to be in a healthy state.

It was now a patient wait. A local resident told of middle-of-the-night reconnaissance rides by one of the teams – she wasn't sure which one, but they had a green car. Whilst I played 'Guess the team', a flurry of police escort motorcyclists arrived,

followed by the first breakaway of riders with UK-based professional Kristian House at the fore. They didn't seem to be suffering too much as they flew by. This apparent lack of effort was confirmed by the Sky-led chasing peleton behind: there was plenty of chatting going on and, towards the back and on the steepest part of the climb, Garmin-Sharp rider Jack Bauer amused the crowd and his peers by riding up doing a wheelie.

17. SUCCOMB'S HILL

Difficulty	◉◉◉◉◉◉◉◉○○○
Distance	0.61km
Av. Gradient	12.2%
Max. Gradient	25%
Height Gain	75m
Start Point	At turn-off from roundabout where Godstone Road meets Croydon Road, follow road marked Succomb's Hill
Local Cafés	Café Bambino, 24 Croydon Road, Caterham CR3 6QB ☎ 01883 331333

This notorious climb just outside the town of Caterham in Surrey, is short and steep with an average gradient of 12% including a thigh-screaming section of 25% gradient towards the top and another hard ramp early on. It is always a difficult test, even with fresh legs at the start of a ride.

Located 2 kilometres north of Caterham, Succomb's Hill leads off the main roundabout where Godstone Road (A22) meets Croydon Road, taking you in the direction of Warlingham.

Coming off the roundabout, you have about 60 metres to get prepared, before the road veers sharply to the right and heads to the skies. You quickly drop into the big sprocket (the lowest you've got, 34 × 27) and it's

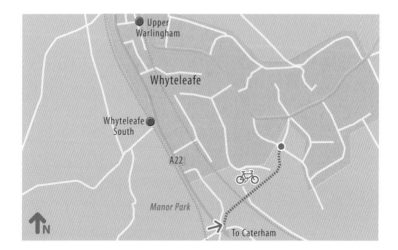

out of the saddle as this first section hits 14–15% with the road ramping up and over the railway tracks. It is a two-lane road but it can get busy at times, so some caution is required with positioning throughout the climb. Once over this first test it eases somewhat as the road winds through a series of S-bends. For the next 200 metres it sits at a pretty hard 10–11%, but you can just about keep the gear turning whilst seated.

Passing the tall pine trees on your left, the next challenge presents itself as you reach a very sharp hairpin left, and as the gradient hits a gruelling 1 in 4, you are straight out of the saddle here for one last, lung-burning effort. The road is narrow and you need to be mindful of your line as oncoming vehicles may be swinging wide on this sharp bend. It will be really hurting by now but keep strong as it is perhaps 70 further metres of intense pushing before you crest the summit – before the gradient relents and you can catch your breath as you approach the turn-off to Narrow Lane, where a bench has been kindly placed (possibly by a cyclist).

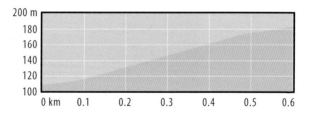

18. WOODHILL LANE

Difficulty	◐◐◑○○○○○○○
Distance	2.51km
Av. Gradient	3.2%
Max. Gradient	13%
Height Gain	81m
Start Point	Junction of B2128 and Woodhill Lane
Local Cafés	The Speckledy Hen Deli and Café, Shamley Green, Guildford GU5 0UB ☎ 01483 894567

This quiet lane, somewhat off the beaten track, starts from the idyllic rural setting of Shamley Green, and has a relatively gentle ascent, gaining 82 metres in elevation over 2.5 twisting, leafy kilometres. During the ascent you will ride past some prime Surrey real estate as you wind up towards Farley Green. The climb is situated about 5 kilometres northwest of the large village of Cranleigh, in the Surrey Hills Area of Outstanding Natural Beauty.

From the village green alongside the B2128, turn onto the road named Woodhill Lane. The first section snakes gently along beyond the cricket pitch and the first kilometre shouldn't cause too many problems as it barely rises above 2% gradient. After 800 metres you pass the right turn to Stroud Lane, and continue straight on,

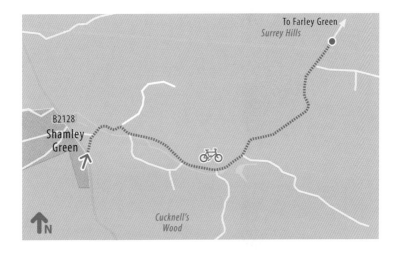

passing a second right turn marked Madgehole Lane. The gradient now begins to rise slightly towards 6%. On your left, there appears to be an enormous Christmas tree plantation; take care here as the road really narrows and on occasions you cannot always see oncoming traffic, though cars are few and far between.

At the 2 kilometre point having passed the tall pine trees on your right hand side and then the quaint farmhouse, the road chicanes and it then rears up to a much more challenging gradient of 12–13%. Shifting to a gear of 39 × 25, you can get out of the saddle to push through this tough final 250 metres into the woods. Round a right hander and the end is near. As you see the bridle path on both sides of the road, you have reached the high point at 142 metres and there's a chance to relax. Continuing on will take you to Farley Green and then Shere, where more climbing can be found if you wish. Alternatively, descend back into Shamley Green to find the nearest point of refreshment at The Speckledy Hen Deli and Café, where you can get a fine cup of coffee.

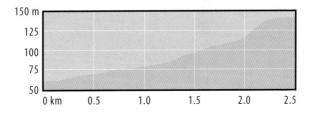

Butser Hill, see overleaf.

19. BUTSER HILL

Difficulty	◎◎◎◎◎◎◐○○○
Distance	2.3km
Av. Gradient	5.8%
Max. Gradient	15%
Height Gain	134m
Start Point	Alongside Upper Parsonage Farm Bed & Breakfast on Harvesting Lane
Local Cafés	The Beech Café, The Sustainability Centre, Droxford Road, East Meon ☎ 01730 823755

This climb on the South Downs, 5 kilometres southwest of Petersfield, leads you all the way up to the telecom tower in the Queen Elizabeth Country Park via a lovely quiet (although at times particularly challenging) lane. In this instance we have started the climb from alongside Upper Parsonage Farm (also known as the middle of nowhere), although for ease of locating you could start at the junction of Oxenbourne Lane and Harvesting Lane and cycle the gentle rolling kilometre beforehand.

Heading in a southwesterly direction along Harvesting Lane we start the description next to the B&B farmhouse (Upper Parsonage). The first 200 metres snakes

around gently until you reach the canopy of trees. Before you know it, you are scrambling for your lowest gears for a short drag. Back briefly into the open, the view of the task ahead is obvious, with the tower glistening at the top of Butser Hill. The road goes straight on for another 100 metres

before it veers sharply to the right past a chalky outcrop, and as you round the bend it's immediately out of the saddle to keep the gear turning over. Unfortunately the gradient doesn't let up for the next half a kilometre and it's a real test for the legs as there is no respite. The sweeping countryside falls away on your right hand side and keeps you from looking up at the road ahead (which looks as bad as it feels). Keep going until you reach the three distinctive trees on the roadside on the right; here I can confirm the worst is over.

At the T-junction turn left (Hogs Lodge Lane/South Downs Way) and onto the single lane with yellow markings. It's a false flat for a few precious moments, your legs are delighted and a wonderful panorama opens up.

Go through the opened gate to the park (this is locked at 8pm) and follow the road with caution through the car park. Stay on the road to the right as it sweeps upwards. If the legs aren't feeling it yet, they will now as you struggle out of the saddle for the last 100 metres to the gate and the very end of the road!

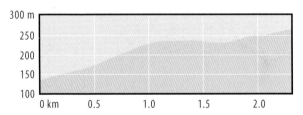

20. STONER HILL

Difficulty	⊙⊙⊙⊙⊙◔○○○○
Distance	2.41km
Av. Gradient	5.7%
Max. Gradient	14%
Height Gain	138m
Start Point	At crossroads with Church Road and Ridge Common Lane
Local Cafés	Folly Tree Tea Rooms, Folly Lane, Petersfield GU31 4AU ☎ 01730 267432

This climb just outside the village of Steep, in the South Downs, has a real mountain pass feel to it, with its longer, gentler gradient and its sweeping bends through beautiful woodland. In fact this part of Hampshire is known as 'Little Switzerland'. It is probably as good a training climb as you will find in the South East if you are planning a trip to the Alps or Pyrenees, though obviously at only 2.5 kilometres long you would need to ride it numerous times on repeat to replicate the distance of a continental climb. It climbs a total of 138 metres at an average of 4.7%.

The climb starts at the crossroads of Church Road and Ridge Common Lane, about 2 kilometres north of Petersfield, and heads in a northwesterly direction. There is a

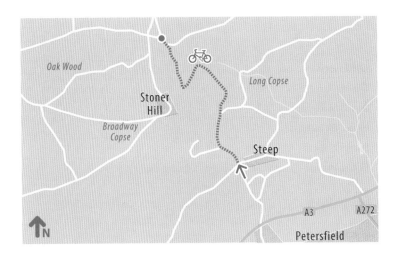

pub here (Cricketers Inn) and a bike shop (Owens Cycles). The first 300 metres is a very gentle introduction at around 3% and then as the road veers to the right, you can see the vast woodland ahead and there is a section of harder gradient to grind through which continues until you pass the turning to Ashford Lane on the right. A mid-range gear should be sufficient. From here the road sweeps into the dense canopy of the Ashford Hangers. Through a long left-hander, you may need to power out of the saddle but otherwise you can stay seated if the legs are feeling fresh. After approximately 1.5 kilometres, there is a break in the tree cover and a levelling of the gradient for 200 metres of respite, but then you hit a tight right-hand bend (beware of traffic swinging wide here) and the gradient and camber requires an extra push.

The gradient eases again after 50 metres and you can get into a good rhythm as the remaining half a kilometre gently chicanes to the summit at High Cross Lane. About 100 metres further on is the Trooper Inn if you fancy a pub lunch; if you'd prefer cake, head back to Folly Tree Tea Rooms in Petersfield.

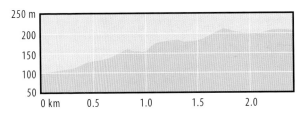

21. KNIGHTS HILL

Difficulty	◉ ◉ ◉ ◉ ◉ ◉ ○ ○ ○ ○
Distance	2.01km
Av. Gradient	4.7%
Max. Gradient	12%
Height Gain	95m
Start Point	From village of Charlton and junction with Charlton Road
Local Cafés	St Martins Tearooms, St Martins Street, Chichester PO19 1NP ☎ 01243 786715

This lovely little climb, situated about 6 kilometres north of Chichester on the South Downs, takes you from the pretty village of Charlton via a hedge-lined ascent onto Charlton Down, which borders the edge of Goodwood racecourse. It's a gradual gradient averaging around 5%, from 64 metres elevation up to 139 metres, on a very quiet single-track road.

From the village of Charlton, turn onto Knights Hill (clearly signposted). The initial 400 metres eases gradually through the outskirts of the pretty thatched cottage village. As you pass the left turn continue on straight ahead. With the somewhat view-spoiling electricity pylon in your sights, the terrain opens out and you can see the road far into the distance clinging to the

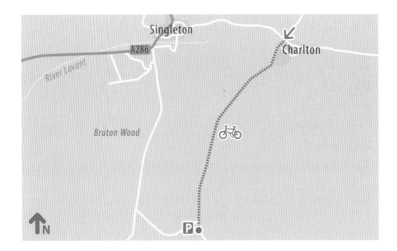

edge of the escarpment. With rolling fields around you it is a steady 11–12% gradient for the next 300 metres or so and with a heavy road surface, standing on the pedals may help you overcome this one difficult section. The pleasant scenery acts as a good distraction if it does start to hurt here. It then eases to around 5% and you can see the road now following along the ridge. The road becomes narrow in parts so keep tucked in if any traffic is approaching; there are regular passing places.

Although the gradient is far easier, this next kilometre can feel very exposed and with an unhelpful wind can be a real struggle. Looking over to your left the grand-stands of the racecourse at Goodwood come into view and you can take in the fabulous rolling countryside too.

Continuing at a good tempo (wind direction permitting) you reach the car park to your left and the junction with the main road at Kennel Hill, where you can take a breather and enjoy the view behind you. Turning left onto Kennel Hill will take you down into Chichester where you can get a bite at St Martins Tearooms.

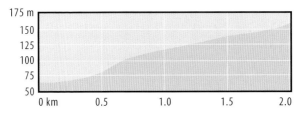

22. WATERSHIP DOWN

Difficulty	◎◎◎◎◎◖○○○○
Distance	1.49km
Av. Gradient	6.2%
Max. Gradient	12%
Height Gain	92m
Start Point	Crossroads with Ecchinswell Road, East of Sydmonton
Local Cafés	Emma's Coffee Shop, 3a Swan Street, Kingsclere, Newbury RG20 5PP ☎ 07449 307519

The hill that inspired the best-selling book is found about 3 kilometres west of the large village of Kingsclere, on the northern fringe of Hampshire. There is something quite charming about the scenery on this little climb, certainly, but I can't say I saw a single rabbit the whole time (possibly I scared them off with my asthmatic wheezing). Starting through a corridor of horse chestnut trees, the very quiet road gradually winds up through an eerily dark wooded section before summiting up on the downs with a feeling of peaceful solitude.

The ascent begins about 1 kilometre south of the village of Ecchinswell (follow Ecchinswell Road and at crossroads go straight over, signposted Ashley Warren). The

first part of this road leading up to Watership Down actually has a few metres of downhill to act as a run up, plus it gives you an opportunity to enjoy the clear view of the down. It is only after about 400 metres that you begin climbing. There are a few patches of gravel on this lower section.

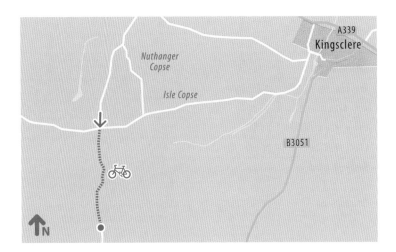

Just before you reach the slight left-hand bend the gradient touches 5% and as the single-lane road chicanes ahead of you it starts to steepen further. Suddenly you are up out of the saddle standing on the pedals for a difficult 100 metre section before it eases again and you can rest the legs. Entering deeper into the woods you are struck by how quiet it is, hardly a car is seen and you may well have the road all to yourself.

Following a right-hander there is a gentler gradient, you can shift down a gear or two, but without warning you are reversing the gear selection as you encounter a 10% ramp – the slope ahead looks deceptively easy but as you climb out of the saddle it steepens to around 1 in 7 for 80 metres. Leaving the darkness of the woods you come out onto the downs and the view of rolling farmland can be enjoyed, there's just a slight rise now to the top and a maximum elevation of 210 metres.

Pop to Emma's Coffee Shop in Kingsclere for an all-day breakfast, pastie or pie (no bunnies included).

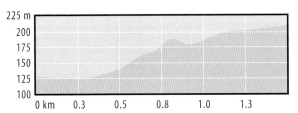

23. BLACKGANG

Difficulty	⊙⊙⊙⊙⊙⊙⊙⊙○○
Distance	1.48km
Av. Gradient	5.7%
Max. Gradient	12%
Height Gain	89m
Start Point	Church Place junction
Local Cafés	Botanic Gardens, Undercliff Drive, Ventnor PO38 1UL ☎ 01983 855397

Anyone who has had the pleasure of cycling on the Isle of Wight will no doubt praise the quiet roads and the great scenery; it is definitely worth a trip over (even for the

day) and for the princely sum of £8 you can take the one-hour ferry crossing with your bike. The southwest corner of the island possesses a couple of testing climbs including this one, which starts in the village of Chale and follows Blackgang Road at an average gradient of 6.4%. The climb described here starts as you enter the village of Chale; however, you may well have already endured many miles of gradual drag along Military Road if you approach from further up the A3055 coastal road from the direction of Brighstone.

The climb starts just as you pass the church, alongside junction with Church Place. The gradient starts at around 5%

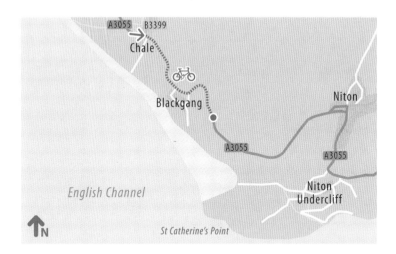

but then gradually increases up to 8%. Watch out for a few potholes on the lower section. Going around a left-hand bend the gradient eases slightly and you can enjoy the sea view away to your right.

Approaching a roundabout, the gradient starts to bite again, varying between 7% and 12%. Stay to the left here (unless you need emergency cake at the Ship Ashore tea rooms – off to right at roundabout but down a steep descent with only one way back). It really feels like a difficult drag: you can stay in the saddle but be prepared to be in this for the long haul (a 39 × 25 should be adequate). With open moorland to your left, the ascent stays at a pretty consistent 8% for the final 400 metres.

Passing a car park on the right (with an opportunity to rest and check out the sea view again) the road follows a couple of sweeping bends before straightening out to reveal the last metres to the summit. It's quite a relief to go over the top and for a reward there's a nice long descent to Niton. Continue on to Ventnor, where the Botanic Gardens (just off the A3055) have a welcoming café.

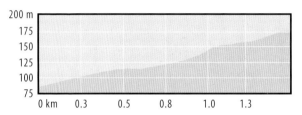

24. WROXALL DOWN

Difficulty	⊙⊙⊙⊙⊙⊙⊙○○
Distance	3.7km
Av. Gradient	6.1%
Max. Gradient	25%
Height Gain	224m
Start Point	Alongside Picardie Hotel on Esplanade
Local Cafés	Besty & Spinky's Café, Ocean Blue Quay, Eastern Esplanade, Ventnor, Isle of Wight PO38 1JR ☎ 01983 857 444

The second ascent on the Isle of Wight is this tough and unforgiving climb, taking you from the seaside hustle and bustle of the esplanade at Ventnor, following a series of switchbacks through the outskirts of the town. It then finishes with one last leg-burning section in the relative wilderness of Wroxall Down. The route is quite convoluted but well worth the effort!

The start point is adjacent to the Picardie Hotel on the Esplanade, with the beach just metres below you. Right from the off it is an energy-sapping climb, with the first ramp leading to a tight right-hand switchback. As you swing round there is an ominous sign warning of 25% gradients. It looks like a wall straight ahead but it is short lived: it soon eases as it winds narrowly between houses before again you hit another switchback and into your lowest gear for a steeper 1 in 4 ramp. Once you crest this short,

sharp shock you approach a T-junction. Turn left here. Continue for 80 metres and then turn right (with caution) onto the imaginatively named Zig Zag Road.

After 100 metres turn left (still following Zig Zag Road). It is a slightly easier gradient as you negotiate these few turns and then after another 100 metres the road turns off to the right,

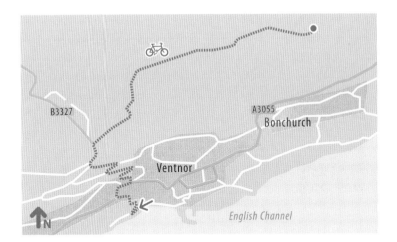

and you are riding up what looks like a residential street. There is a short section of 5% to ease the legs but as the road bends left you encounter another hard section.

Soon you come to the end of Zig Zag Road; turn left onto Ocean View Road and simply keep going upwards! At around the 1.5 kilometre mark you must make a right turn onto Down Lane (it's easy to miss so look out for the pelican crossing and it's 50 metres before that). Passing a few houses either side, the road then becomes a single-track lane and you are suddenly a world away from the buzz of traffic, as you approach Wroxall Down. Unfortunately this is where it really ramps up, in an unforgiving fashion, as you are out of the saddle keeping the pedals turning with weakening legs. It hits a nasty gradient of almost 20% at the 2 kilometre mark.

Once over the cattle grid, the worst is thankfully over and after a long false flat there is just the very gradual rise up to the end of the road at Ventnor Radar station, if you want to get a few more metres of ascent. With luck you will have a fantastic view out to sea. Or you might just see mist. Descend back (watching for walkers and oncoming traffic) to Ventnor and enjoy a cappuccino at Besty and Spinky's Café.

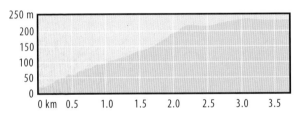

25. SAILOR'S LANE

Difficulty	◉◉◉○○○○○○○
Distance	2.8km
Av. Gradient	3.7%
Max. Gradient	10%
Height Gain	103m
Start Point	At crossroads with Corhampton/Stake's Lane and Sailor's Lane
Local Cafés	Tazzina, High Street, West Meon GU32 1LJ ☎ 01730 829882

An absolute gem of a cycling road in the South Downs, about 4 kilometres northwest of Bishops Waltham, this long ascent (almost 3 kilometres) takes you up to Beacon Hill for a reward of some great views over the Hampshire Basin. It's not the kind of hill that makes you chew on your handlebars; barely going above 10% gradient, it is far gentler than some other hills described in this book. It does provide over 100 metres of elevation gain but equally provides a virtually traffic-free environment and some blissful cycling.

Leaving Bishops Waltham on the B3035 and heading towards Corhampton, you will find the start of Sailor's Lane just off Corhampton Lane/Stake's Lane heading west. Turning onto Sailor's Lane, the first section of this long, gradual ascent takes you through an open, high-hedged wall and you can keep a good tempo in a mid-range

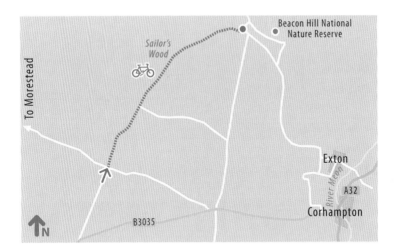

gear as the road snakes through a series of S-bends. It's a narrow, single lane through sections of very lush woodland and it is beautifully quiet, a real pleasure to be riding along.

There is a slight rise in gradient as the road veers to the right and into the shade of the trees. For the next half a kilometre you can maintain a brisk pace, with the woodland to your left and the road taking a route straight on. Encountering the next bend off to the right the cadence quickens over a short stretch of false flat with glimpses of the rolling hills, before returning to the gradual ascent.

Over the next 700 metres the gradient gradually increases, not dramatically, but enough to start feeling it as your heart rate also climbs. Leaving the cover of trees, the landscape to the right comes into full view over this next 80 metre stretch. Swiftly back under the cover of the trees, the road veers sharply to the left and finally you are out of the saddle to power over this one last ramp touching a little over 10% and up to the summit and the T-junction with Beacon Hill Lane.

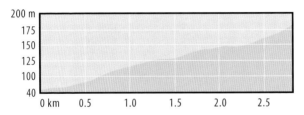

26. PHEASANT'S HILL

Difficulty	⊘⊘⊘⊘⊘⊘◯◯◯◯
Distance	1.24km
Av. Gradient	6.7%
Max. Gradient	15%
Height Gain	83m
Start Point	Alongside United Reformed Church just before left turn (Bottom Hill)
Local Cafés	Hambleden has a shop/café on village square ☎ 01491 571201

This climb, in the scenic Chiltern Hills, starts about 1.5 kilometres north of the idyllic village of Hambleden, Buckinghamshire (the village has been used as a location for films such as *Chitty Chitty Bang Bang* and the remake of *The Avengers*). It is a lovely cycling road with a testing start, a little breather section around halfway before the gradient rises again to bite as you approach the top.

We start this description from alongside the stone wall of the United Reformed Church, just on the outskirts of Hambleden (not the main church in the

centre of the village). Straight away the road swings round sharply to the right so be wary of oncoming traffic. You then ride past the turn off for Bottom Hill, and continue upwards past the row of cottages on the left. It is around 8% but it's not enough to necessitate getting out of the saddle.

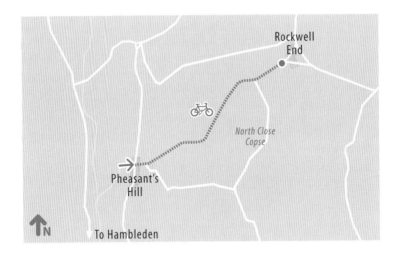

After about 400 metres there is an S-bend and the slope eases for a while, as you pass woodland and then a corn field on your left-hand side. As the hill name suggests, you may well also see a large gathering of pheasants, some with anti-social behaviour, so watch out for kamikaze birds (particularly if you decide to ride back down). Soon you will have a nice 100 metre section of false flat to enjoy before you start climbing again.

Now as the road winds gently upwards, the road narrows and it soon starts to increase in gradient. Reaching for the shifters with legs starting to smart, a jump out of the saddle may be required as it hits 11% at the half kilometre point for about 100 metres and then rises further to around 15% for another 80 metres. Keep pushing as it soon eases, and you can drop down a couple of gears as you roll over the top; at an elevation of 145 metres you can enjoy the best of the Buckinghamshire countryside around you.

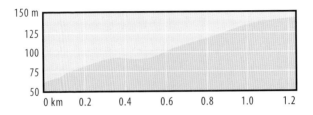

27. DUDLEY LANE

Difficulty	◉◉◉◉◉◉◉◉○○
Distance	1.77km
Av. Gradient	7.3%
Max. Gradient	17%
Height Gain	129m
Start Point	At junction of Dudley Lane and Skirmett Road
Local Cafés	Hambleden has a shop/café on village square ☎ 01491 571201

Located in the Chiltern Hills, this wonderful (if that is the right word) climb is less than 3 kilometres away from Pheasant's Hill, described earlier. From the village of Hambleden, head north up Skirmett Road (towards Skirmett) and at the next cross-roads you come to, Dudley Lane is the single-lane track off to the left. From the base

of the climb the lower slopes follow the hedge-lined farmland, and the relatively open landscape reveals the rollercoaster gradient of the ascent. It looks a bit scary, to be frank, especially with the seemingly ever-present red kites hovering overhead (encouraging some speedier pedalling).

It is a very narrow and quiet back road but beware of oncoming traffic for the entirety, as it's easy to stray wide on some of the steeper curves. There are also stones on some sections.

The first 200 metres eases you into things at around 5–6%, as you go through a series of S-bends, but this very swiftly becomes 11% and the start of a

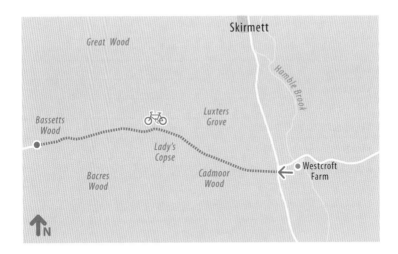

real test. As you shift to your lowest gears (39 × 28 would probably suffice; 34 × 28 makes life easier) you are soon on a ramp of 17% and it is back-breaking stuff for the next 250 metres, that is until you reach a big left-hander and it hurts some more.

Once you reach the woods, there is some short relief whilst you get your breath back but it's a respite of only 50 metres before the road climbs steeply again and you are out of the saddle once more, though the road looks deceptively gentler in gradient.

There are a few potholes in this section and the road surface is generally poor so watch your line. As you pass the vineyards, the hard bit is over. On your right you pass the Chiltern Valley Brewery (try to resist the immense temptation here) and then there is a gentle incline of around 3% as you snake another 700 metres through serene woodland to the summit at 201 metres and an overall elevation gain of 129 metres. This last section serves as a warm-down after what can only be described as a killer climb!

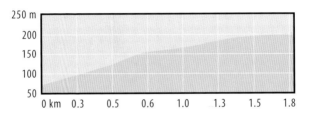

28. KOP HILL

Difficulty	⊘⊘⊘⊘⊘⊘⊘⊘○○
Distance	1.15km
Av. Gradient	9.1%
Max. Gradient	20%
Height Gain	105m
Start Point	At junction with New Road/Brimmers Road and Kop Hill
Local Cafés	Anton Hazelle's Artisan Chocolaterie Café, 40 High Street, Princes Risborough HP27 0AX ☎ 01844 273993

More famous as a climb used for motorsports, and one of the oldest hill climbs in the UK, you may struggle to come close to the 22.8 second record ascent on an engine-less cycle – particularly as it has a vicious bite just over halfway, where it touches 1 in 5. It may be short, but it is a real test for the legs, having an average gradient of almost 10%.

This brute lies less than a kilometre southeast of the town of Princes Risborough. From the (testing) rise up New Road you turn onto Kop Hill and the treat in store is in clear view!

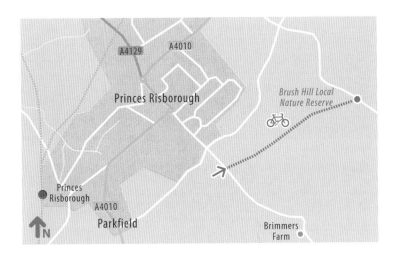

It starts off at a gentle 2% for about 200 metres, then the road gently curves to the left and under the canopy of trees. Here it starts to get tough pretty quickly as it hits 8% and continues to burn as it steepens further towards 17% for about 100 hellish metres. Thankfully it diminishes back to a gradient of 1 in 10, but looking up it is over way too soon as another hard ramp approaches, and you are standing on the pedals over a 15% incline. The road gives little chance for finding a rhythm, as ahead there is another short 'platform' of relief before it crests up once more. Now as it reaches its maximum grade touching 20% it really starts to hurt and you realize why this is more popular with racing cars. In your lowest gear (34 × 27 would be a good option for the average climber) you are fighting to keep moving, but keep the faith through this last push over 80 metres of struggle as you crest the wall. An easier gradient awaits and you can get your breath back on the final 150 metres up to the top and the junction with St Peters Lane. If you want to be King of the Mountains, you would be looking at a time of a tad over 3 minutes for the 105 metre vertical ascent.

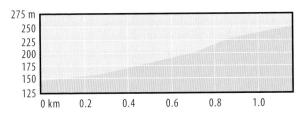

29. IVINGHOE BEACON

Difficulty	⬤⬤◉◉○○○○○○
Distance	2.16km
Av. Gradient	3.8%
Max. Gradient	7%
Height Gain	82m
Start Point	At junction with B489 Tring Road, signposted Ivinghoe Beacon
Local Cafés	CuriosiTEA Rooms, at the Old School, 2 High Street ☎ 07775 831153

Situated just over a kilometre northeast of Ivinghoe in Buckinghamshire, this picturesque climb corkscrews around the chalky grassland of the beacon, revealing fantastic sprawling views of the Buckinghamshire and neighbouring Hertfordshire countryside. It is, to be fair, not the most gruelling of cycling hills at an average of just over 4%, but it is one of the quietest and more scenic rides to be found in the area, passing as it does, through National Trust owned land.

The road up to the beacon turns off the busy B489 (be careful along this stretch

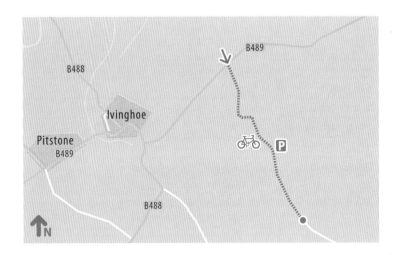

as vehicles do pass at considerable speed), and soon the contrast is striking as this quiet single lane stretches up through remote countryside. After 50 metres you cross a cattle grid and settle into a consistent tempo as the gradient barely goes over 5%. The road sweeps to the right and then sharply to the left as you channel through the grassy escarpment, the gradient increasing ever so slightly.

The view opens out in front of you after around 600 metres and far ahead you can make out the Whipsnade Zoo White Lion carved into the chalk. With the road turning to the right and with legs still spinning at a good cadence, the road ahead straightens and soon you enter a short section of woodland and with it a subtle increase in the gradient to 6%, and then to 7%. Passing the car park on your left and with a great view to momentarily take in, the ascent eases to around 2–3%. Going over a second cattle grid, there's a short false flat for around 200 metres before it climbs again, albeit at a nice leg-loosening gradient of 3%. There is no official summit point but it peaks at a 251 metre elevation just after the 2 kilometre mark.

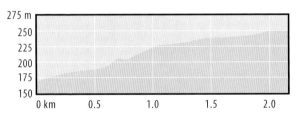

30. WHITCHURCH HILL

Difficulty	⦾⦾⦾⦾⦾⦾⦾◯◯◯
Distance	1.02km
Av. Gradient	8.5%
Max. Gradient	14%
Height Gain	87m
Start Point	Adjacent to Manor Road, just after Whitchurch Bridge
Local Cafés	Little Henry's Café, 3–5 Reading Road, Pangbourne RG8 7LR ☎ 01189 842246

This ascent, in a very scenic part of the Chilterns, is pretty short at just over a kilometre, but averages almost 8% with a particularly challenging finale. Being within 7 kilometres of Streatley Hill (see hill climb 31) it is easy to combine the two – not that your legs will necessarily agree.

Leaving the large village of Pangbourne and heading north across the River

Thames (on B471) you pass over Whitchurch Bridge, where there's a toll for motorists but cyclists can pass through gratis.

The climb starts in earnest a further 200 metres along the High Street adjacent to Manor Road; beginning at a gradient below 4%. After 150 metres the road cuts tightly through a passageway of houses; proceed with caution,

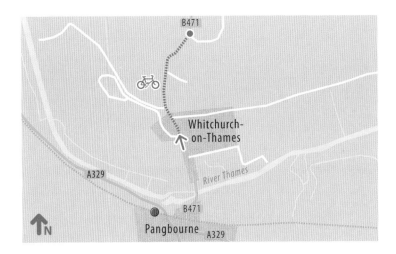

as you must give priority to oncoming traffic for the next 60 metres. At this point you start to drop down through the gears as the gradient creeps up to 8–9%. Once past the last remaining village houses, the road opens up and it snakes high into dense woodland. Climbing steadily through the trees it averages around 9% and you can stay seated with a gear combination of 39 × 25 (that's not to say it doesn't hurt). Continuing along this straight section of road you pass the First World War memorial on your left and alongside it a bench that I'm quite sure calls out my name. The gradient starts to bite now as it rises above 13–14%, and as the road bends to the right it seems to kick up again. Shifting down a couple of gears and getting out of the saddle is required to keep the momentum with ever tiring quads. The road surface is a little heavy here which saps the energy even further but as you ride through a couple more gentle bends, and after 250 metres of perseverance, the end is finally in sight.

Passing the sign for Whitchurch Hill, the climbing is behind you (elevation 134 metres). Be careful if you stop here, as the road is narrow with high verges.

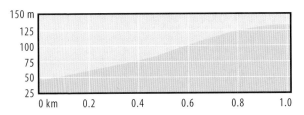

31. STREATLEY HILL

Difficulty	◉◉◉◉◉◉◉◉○○
Distance	0.94km
Av. Gradient	11.2%
Max. Gradient	17%
Height Gain	105m
Start Point	From traffic lights at Reading Road, alongside Bull Inn
Local Cafés	Pierreponts, High Street, Goring, Reading RG8 9AB ☎ 01491 874464

Regularly featuring in the Tour of Britain cycle race (as a Category 2 climb), this tough hill is relatively short but very steep. Avoiding this hill is not a modern phenomenon: in

the late nineteenth century the English poet Joseph Ashby-Sterry declared: 'And when you're here, I'm told that you should mount the hill and see the view; and gaze and wonder, if you'd do its merits most completely: the air is clear, the day is fine, the prospect is, I know, divine – but most distinctly I decline to climb the hill at Streatley.'

The hill in question follows the B4009 as you pass out of the village of Goring. Crossing over the Thames, there is a slight rise as you approach the crossroads and the A329; go straight over and past the 'olde worlde' Bull pub. We start our description here.

The first stretch alongside the pub is a narrow single lane so be

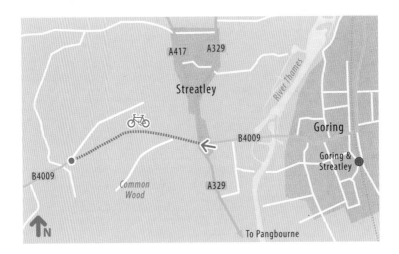

wary of traffic turning off the main road. It then widens to two lanes and for the next 200 metres it is a 7–8% gradient and so far so good. But very soon it takes an unpleasant turn for the worse: the road deviates to the left and you are scrambling for your lowest gear (34 × 27 would be a safe option, particularly with tired legs). What you now have ahead of you is a seemingly endless slog upwards through woodland with the gradient staying between 15% and 20% for the next 400 metres. Standing on the pedals and with as much positivity as you can muster, ignore the leg burning as best as you can!

Passing a residential driveway on the left you can just make out a flattening of the gradient 80 metres up ahead and this is where the hurt ends. Passing the car park on your right, you can drop down a couple of gears and recover your composure at the summit (which here is a distinctly anti-climactic bridlepath). Crossing back over the river towards Goring will take you past Pierreponts Café (next to the Royal Mail sorting office) on the High Street.

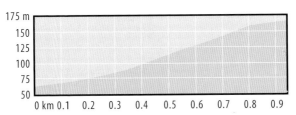

32. FACCOMBE HILL

Difficulty	⊙⊙⊙⊙⊙⊙○○○○
Distance	1.68km
Av. Gradient	5.9%
Max. Gradient	15%
Height Gain	99m
Start Point	Equidistant between the villages of East Woodhay and West Woodhay, (approx. 1km northeast of East Woodhay)
Local Cafés	Courtyard Café, Thatchers Yard, Kintbury RG17 9TR ☎ 01488 658717

This climb, up to the highest chalk down in the UK, is set in the heart of rural West Berkshire. It has the familiar theme of a gentle start, rising a bit in the middle then trying to finish off your legs as you hit the final steeper section. It does offer something of a pay back with some beautiful views of the valley and on a clear day you can see for miles.

The start is a little hard to describe, being somewhat in the middle of nowhere, but that is a big part of the appeal. If you happen upon a car on this climb you have probably been fairly unlucky, although of course you should be prudent as the lane is particularly narrow. In terms of location the start point is equidistant between the villages of East Woodhay and West Woodhay, approximately 4 kilometres south of the village of Kintbury.

Setting off on the single-track lane, there is ample time to get

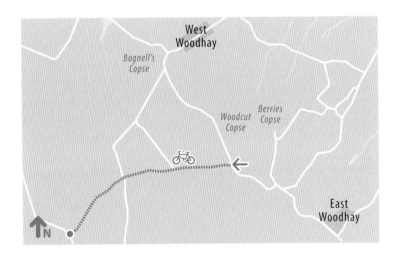

warmed up as the first kilometre averages a very sedate 3%. As you pootle along enjoying the virtually traffic-free road your mind is free to wander, and then as you pass under the overhanging trees you begin to hit the first rise in incline.

With a chalky scree outcrop on your left you are suddenly climbing at a gradient of 11–13% and most likely out of the saddle here. The landscape around you reveals its glory and rolling hills fall away to your right. Unfortunately there is little time to enjoy the view as it's a case of putting your head down and your back into getting over this long drag of just over 400 metres. In your lowest gear, you will still need to be standing on the pedals as it continues to steepen up to 15%.

With legs and lungs now burning it is quite a relief to get over this stretch; the final 250 metres have just the slightest of gradients and you can sit back and recover as you ride to the T-junction. Turning right here and then right on to Rooksnest will take you on a nice descent into Kintbury where you will find fantastic cakes at the Courtyard Café.

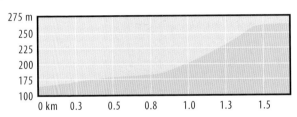

33. QUARRY WOOD

Difficulty	⬤⬤⬤⬤⬤⬤◍◯◯◯
Distance	0.94km
Av. Gradient	6.6%
Max. Gradient	22%
Height Gain	62m
Start Point	Quarry Wood Road, at stone walled bridge before turn off to Quarry Wood
Local Cafés	Burgers Artisian Bakery, The Causeway, Marlow SL7 1NF ☎ 01628 483389

There is some pleasant cycling to be found as you head away from Maidenhead and towards the Chilterns, passing through numerous quaint villages as you follow the course of the River Thames. This tough ascent between Cookham and Marlow has a difficult first 200 metres, as you curve around a steep hairpin, before it continues to sap away at the leg strength on a long, straight drag through Quarry Wood. Nestled on the boundary of Berkshire and Buckinghamshire, it has an average gradient of 6.6%.

It is located about 1 kilometre southeast of Marlow, close to the A404. The

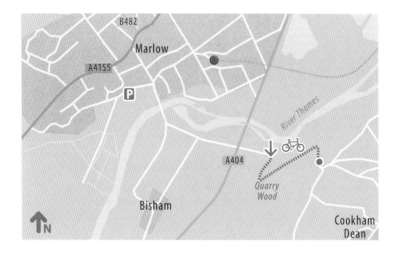

climb starts as you cross the stone walled bridge (Parole Bridge) and just before the left turn (Quarrywood, a cul-de-sac).

There is little opportunity for a warm-up on this one as the road swings immediately to the right, and the gradient hits 6% – rapidly becoming a steady 10%. At the 200-metre point the road bends sharply to the left and it is out of the saddle to power over a very steep camber hitting 22%; a gear of 34 × 27 would be the order of the day. Back into the saddle as you round this bend and the road straightens out ahead of you. There is a slight dip, but only for 50 metres, before the gradient settles again between 8% and 10% for the next 500 metres, on a long straight drag through the trees. Here you can settle into something approaching a rhythm before the road bends sharply to the right, a small push over the rise and you reach the high point of 264 metres and just shy of 100 metres elevation gain, the end point being just as you approach the turn-off to Grubwood Lane and Dean Lane. Retrace your steps and head across the bridge to Marlow for a bite to eat.

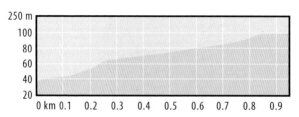

34. UFFINGTON WHITE HORSE

Difficulty	◐◐◐◐◐◐◐○○○
Distance	1km
Av. Gradient	9.7%
Max. Gradient	15%
Height Gain	97m
Start Point	At junction with B4507, opposite Broad Way
Local Cafés	Vale and Downland Museum Café, 19 Church Street, Wantage OX12 8BL ☎ 01235 771447

This fantastic little climb up past the famous escarpment with the Bronze-Age horse carved into the chalky hillside, is to all intents and purposes another cul-de-sac with a car park at the end – which makes it a very traffic-light and enjoyable cycle, almost enough to make you forget your legs are suffering over this 1-in-10 ascent. It is, moreover, one of the more scenic climbs in the South East region.

Situated 6 kilometres south of the town of Faringdon, it branches off from the B4507 directly opposite the road named Broad Way (running south from village of Uffington) though you have no problem seeing where you are about to go. The hill rises majestically and you can see the road cutting a path through the valley. If in doubt still, follow the signs for White Horse.

Heading off on this narrow lane and watching for the patches of gravel along the way the road kicks up almost immediately and within 50 metres you are climbing a gradient between 8% and 10%. Crossing the cattle grid (quite tricky when you are climbing!) the view ahead is spectacular as an S-bend follows the

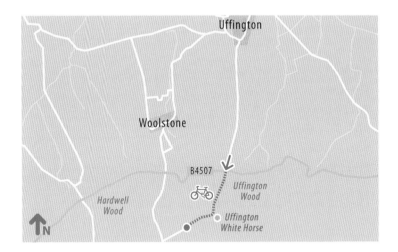

steep grassy banks, the incline now ramps up to 15% and if you are not already in your lowest gear, you soon will be. Around a left-hand bend it eases slightly; to your right the landscape falls away dramatically as the road narrows further.

As the road veers to the right it feels like you are hanging on the edge of the escarpment. On your left-hand side you may catch the tail of the famous white horse, though that is enjoyed better if you stop on the way back down. It is out of the saddle as you power over an 80-metre stretch at 13%; it begins to feel quite exposed here so wind will often be a big factor too. Eventually the gradient relents to around 5% and then for the last 100 metres to the finish drops further to 3% providing much-needed relief. The somewhat underwhelming summit is reached at the car park on the right, where the overwhelming views provide a great reward.

Cream teas can be sought at the farmhouse (signposted) a kilometre down the B4507, though opening hours are limited to weekend afternoons. Failing that, head to the Vale and Downland Museum Café in Wantage.

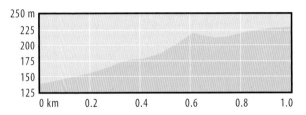

35. BLOWINGSTONE HILL

Difficulty	⊘⊘⊘⊘⊘⊘⊘◯◯◯
Distance	0.71km
Av. Gradient	10.6%
Max. Gradient	14%
Height Gain	75m
Start Point	At junction of B4507 and Blowingstone Hill, south of the village of Kingston Lisle
Local Cafés	Devonia Bakery and Café, 2 Pegasus Court, Lambourn RG17 8XW ☎ 01488 73205

Turning off the B4507 towards Kingston Warren, this short, straight brute nestled in the White Horse Hills (less than 2 kilometres from the Uffington White Horse climb described previously) will certainly test your legs, with an average gradient of over 10%.

The first 60 to 70 metres are not too harsh, but then suddenly you are shifting all the way to the dinner plate sprocket for an abrupt 12–14% ramp, which continues for an unrelenting 150 metres, and you will probably be out of the saddle for this tough start along the tree-lined lane.

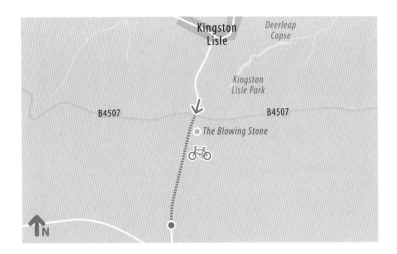

As the road bends ever so slightly to the left, the gradient eases a little and you can remain seated here as the ascent stays at a fairly steady 9% or 10% for the remainder, apart from a cruel 50-metre ramp near the top (a quick dance on the pedals will get you over this and you can drop back down to the saddle). As you pass the gradient warning sign on the right-hand side, and the top at an elevation of 202 metres you can breathe easily again.

Continuing straight on takes you over the Berkshire Downs and towards Lambourn where you face exposed wind-blown roads over what is known as the Valley of the Racehorse (over 2,000 racehorses are trained in this area).

Turning back and descending Blowingstone provides a very fast, exhilarating downhill on a fairly straight road, but beware: the junction approaches very quickly!

Eateries are few and far between but try Devonia Bakery and Café. During the summer months you may be able to get a cream tea (advertised at a roadside farmhouse) along the B4507 towards Uffington White Horse.

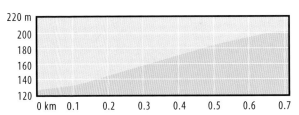

ROCK OF AGES

In the fenced garden of the cottage at the bottom of Blowingstone Hill, you can find a famous lump of sarsen rock known as the blowingstone.

The rock is perforated with numerous holes and, providing you have the lung-capacity of the average Andean hill farmer, you might be able to encourage a deep booming sound that apparently can be heard up to six miles away. Legend has it that King Alfred the Great used this improvised bugle to rally his troops at the nearby Battle of Ashdown. The stone is also mentioned in the Thomas Hughes' novel Tom Brown's Schooldays.

The stone was supposedly brought down from near the site of the Uffington White Horse on the Ridgeway in the eighteenth century and rested outside the local hostelry for many years (where the landlord's party piece was to produce a loud note from it). The pub subsequently became the Blowingstone Inn and though it later relocated to the village of Kingston Lisle (opposite Blowingstone Hill) the stone remained. The original pub, in time, became the cottage you now see at the bottom of the hill.

Those who fancy trying their luck in getting a tune from the stone would be advised doing so after they have successfully ridden to the top of the hill and had a rest!

36. WATLINGTON HILL

Difficulty	⦿⦿⦿⦿⦿⦿◯◯◯◯
Distance	2.2km
Av. Gradient	5.7%
Max. Gradient	16%
Height Gain	125m
Start Point	Alongside turning to Watlington Care Home
Local Cafés	The Bread Bin, 4 High Street, Watlington OX49 5PS ☎ 01491 613061

This climb in the Chiltern Hills, just outside the pretty village of Watlington, Oxfordshire, rises to an elevation of 241 metres up to the hamlet of Christmas Common. The ascent follows Hill Road, after turning off the B4009 heading southwest from the village. For ease of description, the precise start point here is approximately 400 metres along Hill Road, adjacent to the turn off for Watlington & District Care Home.

The first 200 metres is a gentle gradient, along a dead-straight road through a residential area. It is around 2–3% percent so a good chance to loosen the legs for the long climb ahead up to Christmas Common. You may notice a white triangle (named

the Watlington White Mark) carved into the hillside ahead; this was cut into the chalk in 1764 by a local squire to create the impression that the church of St Leonard had a spire when viewed from his home.

Passing the turn-off to the caravan and camping site to your right, the gradient slowly starts to steepen and as you ride beyond the last

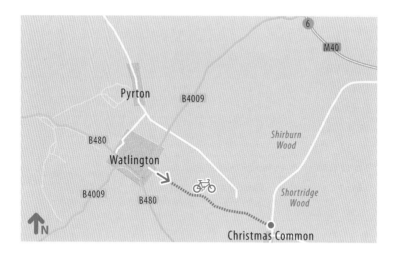

house the road bends to the left and suddenly kicks up to around 16% and it is smartly out of the saddle to keep the momentum over the next 100 metres, until you ride around a sweeping right-hander where it starts to ease. You now enter a section between 8% and 11% but it doesn't really feel a lot easier.

The view starts to open out on your left hand side; as the landscape drops away the odd red kite floats smugly on thermals above, but fortunately here the gradient drops for a much-needed 100 metres of leg recovery. Make the very most of this little section as the next kilometre or so ramps up again to a near constant 10% and it is a war of attrition as legs start to tire.

Passing Watlington Hill Farm on the left, you can be assured that the worst is definitely over. The gradient levels off and apart from a slight rise to the crossroads and the sign for Christmas Common you can coast the final 200 metres.

Return back into Watlington, navigating the complex one-way system for cake and an excellent array of milkshakes at The Bread Bin.

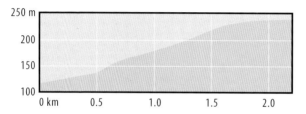

37. ASTON HILL

Difficulty	⊙⊙⊙⊙○○○○○○
Distance	2.7km
Av. Gradient	4.9%
Max. Gradient	9%
Height Gain	131m
Start Point	Junction with B4009, A40 Aston Hill
Local Cafés	The Bread Bin, 4 High Street, Watlington OX49 5PS ☎ 01491 613061

Twisting at a nice steady gradient up through Aston Wood in the Chiltern Hills of Oxfordshire, this climb follows the former main thoroughfare of the A40, which now has more of an eerie feeling of a back road with the M40 being very much within earshot as the hum of traffic cuts through this chalky escarpment. The ascent stays at an almost constant 5% gradient throughout the ascent of close to 3 kilometres, making life easier for the HGVs that were once forced to take this route and for the cyclists that now choose to.

It starts about 5 kilometres northwest of Watlington, Oxfordshire, just after you pass beneath the M40, travelling along the B4009 in the direction of Chinnor. Turning onto the A40, the first 1.5 kilometres snakes along at a fairly gentle gradient. Arcing around a long left-hander, which takes you past a factory on the right-hand side, there follows a section with an overtaking lane. The level of

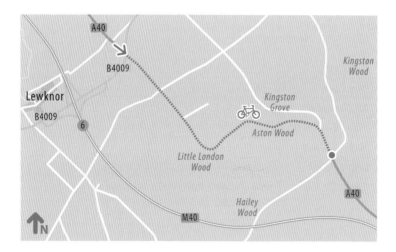

traffic can be surprisingly low with just the occasional passing vehicle, but there are a couple of tight turns in which to be particularly wary of traffic. (The road surface is good so there's no need to weave around potholes.)

With the gradient continuing at this constant 4–5%, you can keep a mid-range gear turning and stay comfortably in the saddle; it really has the feel of an alpine climb. You can make it as easy or hard as you want, to be honest, and it is great for longer interval training, especially if you are in the midst of preparing for the Étape du Tour or Marmotte cycle sportives.

The road continues to snake upwards through the dense woodland and the long effort comes to an end as you pass the sign for Aston Wood and continue to the crossroads approximately 2.7 kilometres in, having reached an elevation of 254 metres.

Turning left at the crossroads here takes you down Kingston Hill (a climb worth tackling if you still feel fresh). Heading back to Watlington will provide a coffee stop at The Bread Bin.

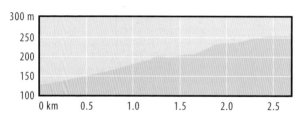

38. SWAINS LANE

Difficulty	⊘⊘⊘⊘⊘⊘○○○○
Distance	0.87km
Av. Gradient	7.7%
Max. Gradient	13%
Height Gain	67m
Start Point	Junction with Chester Road, on Swains Lane
Local Cafés	The Highgate Pantry, 57 Highgate High Street N6 5JX ☎ 020 8340 4747

Well-known amongst cycle commuters living in leafy North London, Swains Lane is one of the few true tests to be found in the capital itself with an average gradient of nearly 8%. It winds unnervingly through Highgate Cemetery (the resting place of Karl Marx) before ramping up dramatically to the affluent village of Highgate.

The climb starts at the junction with Chester Road, to the south of Highgate and avoiding the similarly tough but busier Highgate Hill. It's a fairly gentle introduction for the first 350 metres, with a row of residential buildings on your left and the cemetery to your right, giving you a chance to admire the ivy-clad gothic tombstones and, depending on your state of mind, ponder your own potential mortality on this short but tough climb!

Passing parked cars on the left and negotiating speed bumps, you can continue with a good cadence along this moderate 7% gradient until you reach the entrance to the cemetery on

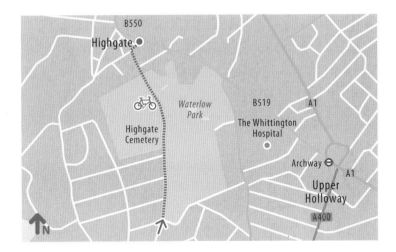

either side and, a little further on, the faded yellow house on the right. Here the road narrows considerably to a single lane and takes a dramatic shift in gradient where it hits around 12–13%; swiftly select your lowest sprocket and be ready to grind this section out. With an imposing wall next to you on the left, you are out of the saddle for the final thigh-bursting 80 metres up this narrow ascent. This section is one-way, so be aware of traffic approaching from behind with the occasional straining London bus.

As you pass the entrance to Waterlow Park on the right, the worst is definitely over and the gradient eases again. A few metres further along the road you pass a communications mast and here it becomes two-way, so proceed with caution. The finish is at the junction with South Grove (directly opposite are toilet facilities) and an elevation of 130 metres.

Turning to the right you will find a plethora of chain cafés but heading left, a little further up Highgate High Street at number 57, you will find The Highgate Pantry with an excellent selection of cakes to satisfy all.

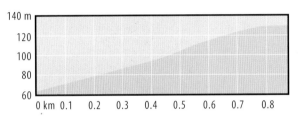

39. MUSWELL HILL

Difficulty	◉◉◉◉◉◉○○○○
Distance	0.73km
Av. Gradient	8.1%
Max. Gradient	12%
Height Gain	59m
Start Point	At junction with Park Road and Priory Road
Local Cafés	Syls Café, 316 Park Road, Muswell Hill N8 8LA ☎ 07712 227000

One for the urban foxes amongst you, this climb is a short, sharp burst of less than 750 metres with an average gradient of over 8%. Along with Swains Lane, it is one of the few decent climbs in the north of the Capital. It is a busy stretch with the usual London traffic so caution is required; however, the majority of the ascent has the relative security of being in a segregated bus lane, though if you are particularly unlucky you may get a bus crawling along behind you (but not as unlucky as the driver of the bus!).

The climb starts at the traffic lights at the junction with Park Road and Priory Road, with Muswell Hill (A504) heading northwest. The first part does not have the protection of the bus lane so be wary of

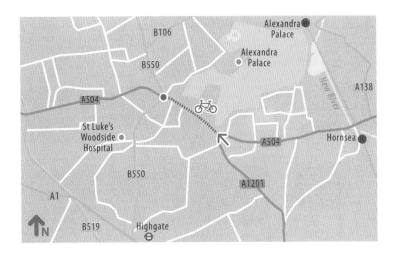

your line on this steady 7% opening stretch passing the entrance to Alexandra Palace on the right. As you reach the bus lane it gradually starts to get steeper, to around 10%. A further 150 metres further on and you pass a bus stop (preferably without a bus to hold you up, so that you can keep your momentum going), the climb starts to bare its teeth now, staying around 1 in 10 and then rising slightly to 12% for a short ramp. A little shimmy out of the saddle will keep you powering up, though the rouleurs will be able to stay seated and grind it out.

Being mindful of vehicles on some of the side roads to your left, you can keep steadily tapping out a rhythm as it now settles at around 8%. As you approach the roundabout, you reach a natural end point as you pause for a gap in the traffic here (it's quite busy). There are quite a few chain cafés around here, or if you prefer to support the smaller local establishments, head back to the start point and try Syls Café for some delicious home-made cakes (including gluten-free). Next door is an interesting little bike shop, Future Cycles.

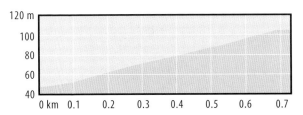

40. ROBINS NEST HILL

Difficulty	◐◐◑○○○○○○○
Distance	1.9km
Av. Gradient	3.7%
Max. Gradient	8%
Height Gain	70m
Start Point	Junction of Robins Nest Hill and B158 (Lower Hatfield Road)
Local Cafés	The Orchid, 64 Station Road, Potters Bar EN6 4HA ☎ 01707 876720

This is one of the few climbs of note in the (seemingly) flat lands of Hertfordshire. It starts alongside the River Lea and rises up to the pretty village of Little Berkhamsted, almost 2 kilometres of really fantastic cycling terrain with some cracking views along the way. The lower section provides more of a test than the far gentler gradient of the last kilometre; at an overall average of around 4% it shouldn't trouble most cyclists.

It is a wonderfully quiet little road and that is the reason for its inclusion here, though it still provides 70 metres of elevation gain so it is by no means a walk in the park.

The climb is located around 5 kilometres southwest of the town of Hertford and branches off from the B158 (Lower Hatfield Road). The road (named Robins Nest Hill) heads due south and the first 100

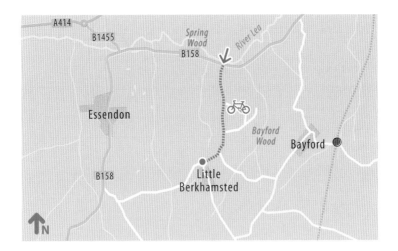

metres start gently before you enter the cover of trees where the gradient slowly begins to rise. The road surface is not the best in places so be mindful of your line.

Going around a long left-hander you reach a section of 6–8% before the road straightens out and you approach the outskirts of the village of Little Berkhamsted. You can now enjoy a lesser gradient and change down through the gears, and looking off to the right you catch a glimpse of the scenic landscape through a clearing.

From here the gradient decreases further, and you pass some very elegant dwellings including the imposing Grade II listed Strattons Tower, a five-storey observation building, recently restored. There is just the occasional car to keep an eye out for but otherwise you can push on at speed over the last kilometre, which is a very subtle 2 3%. The summit, at an elevation of 117 metres, is at the crossroads with Church Road, alongside the memorial to First World War soldiers.

If you are looking for more hills in the area, head further south towards Cuffley for some testing climbs, including Carbone Hill.

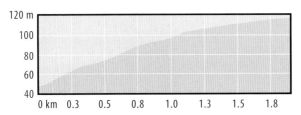

41. WELLINGTON HILL

Difficulty	⊙⊙⊙⊙⊙⊙○○○○
Distance	0.83km
Av. Gradient	6.0%
Max. Gradient	13%
Height Gain	50m
Start Point	At junction of Wellington Hill and Pynest Green Lane
Local Cafés	The Tea Hut

Located in the marvellous cycling territory of Epping Forest is this gentle climb, around 4 kilometres southwest of Waltham Abbey. From Pynest Green Lane it continues in a southwesterly direction, taking you into the western fringe of this beautiful ancient forest.

Turning off Pynest Green Lane onto the single track of Wellington Hill, the road chicanes upwards through this first residential section, initially at a gradient of around 6–7% where you can maintain a reasonable speed. You soon lose momentum, however, as within 60 metres the gradient almost doubles to 12% for the next 80-metre section. Heading into the overhang of the trees, you have a short chance to recover before it once again climbs to 9–10%.

Passing the entrance to High Beech Golf Club, the climbing dramatically eases and relents further as you pass the Duke of Wellington pub on the left, and

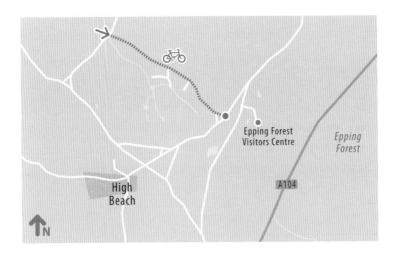

here it is a very modest 3%. Looking up the road though, you can see the next sharp incline as you ride up into the denser woodland. You can stay in the saddle and a gear of perhaps 34 × 23 for this segment, as it remains at a fairly constant 8–9% for the majority, except for a short rise of 13% that you'll probably need to shift down for or power out of the saddle.

Approaching the speed control barrier (there is a 20 mph limit on this road so take it easy!), where you have priority over oncoming traffic, the worst of the climbing is over and you can drop down a couple of gears for this final stretch at a painless 5%, meandering through the peaceful forest. A triangular island in the road signifies the summit and an elevation of 113 metres.

Turning left here and within 50 metres cutting along the path to the right, you will get to the road marked High Beech; next to the Kings Oak pub is a little café (The Tea Hut) – if you can't find it, it is usually hidden behind the numerous groups of motorcyclists who descend here at weekends.

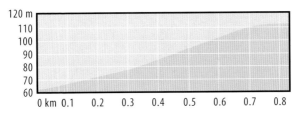

42. NORTH HILL

Difficulty	◎◎◎◎◎◎○○○○
Distance	1.87km
Av. Gradient	4.4%
Max. Gradient	9%
Height Gain	83m
Start Point	At Paper Mill Lock, by river on North Hill
Local Cafés	Old Stables Tea Rooms, Paper Mill Lock, North Hill, Little Baddow, Chelmsford CM3 4BS ☎ 01245 225520

Essex being one of the flatter counties in the South East, the choice of decent climbs is certainly quite limited. But this one, starting alongside the River Chelmer (next to Paper Mill Lock), and taking you up through the village of Little Baddow (to a high point of 98 metres) is quite a good test; mostly because of its length of almost 2 kilometres. It is located about 6 kilometres east of Chelmsford. North Hill can be reached via the B1137 from Mowden Hall Lane.

Beginning at Paper Mill Lock, head in a southerly direction along North Hill. The first 300 metres is virtually flat, then as the road starts to narrow and with

houses on your left, you encounter the first short incline of 8% gradient, but at only 60 metres in length you can up the power to get over it.

It then settles into a pretty steady 4–5% and as the road bends to the left, you approach a built-up area. With cars parked on the

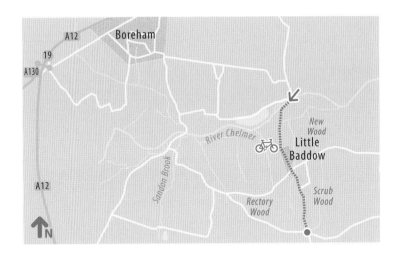

right-hand side of the road, be cautious of oncoming vehicles encroaching on your side of the road.

The road widens a little further up and you can enjoy an easier gradient to get your breath back, but approaching a sweeping right-hander it rises again. This time it is a long, hard drag up a gradient between 8% and 9% and it is here that it really begins to burn. Dropping now into a 34 × 23 (or lower) you should be able to remain in the saddle.

After about 300 metres, be wary again of oncoming traffic passing stationary cars, this time on the left. You ride past a distinctive red ivy-clad cottage and the gradient eases somewhat to a more manageable 6%. There is a short rise to power over and then, as you pass Little Baddow Memorial Hall on your left, the pink house ahead comes into view. This is the summit of the climb, at the crossroads with Spring Elm Lane.

Head back down the hill to the start point at Paper Mill Lock where you will find the Old Stables Tea Rooms and some nice views of the river.

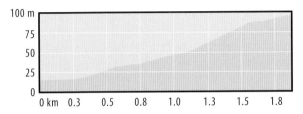

43. YORKS HILL

Difficulty	◎◎◎◎◎◎◎◎◎○
Distance	0.7km
Av. Gradient	12.4%
Max. Gradient	25%
Height Gain	87m
Start Point	Not easy to describe: climb ends at junction opposite Nightingale Lane. Start point just under 700m down the lane!
Local Cafés	Chartwell (National Trust), Mapleton Road, Westerham TN16 IPS ☎ 01732 868381

Yorks Hill has achieved notoriety amongst local cyclists as an ascent bordering on the masochistic. It is used for the Catford CC Hill Climb every October, drawing huge crowds to this shaded, narrow lane to witness some of the best amateur cyclists tackling this unforgiving 'wall'. It is also well known to the many who have ridden the King of the Downs sportive, coming as it does around 90 miles in; it really does separate the men from the boys, many of whom surrender to the steep gradients and are forced to walk.

It is quite hard to find on a map, but it runs almost parallel to Ide Hill Road, although further east nearer to Bough Beech Reservoir (you could approach from this direction as Yorks Hill is signposted).

In order to replicate the Catford CC climb (though continuing down to the farm buildings alongside the huge weeping willow tree will provide an extra 500 metres of distance and 30 metres of climbing), the easiest option is to actually approach from the summit and descend down a little (Yorks Hill is directly opposite Nightingale Lane heading south from Goathurst Common). The climb starts then at a fairly nondescript point 700 metres downhill (you will need to measure this out I'm afraid, as there is no real point of reference other than trees!). From this starting point there are just a few metres of lesser gradient before you are facing a real, hard slog. Selecting your lowest gear (34 × 28), think happy thoughts and don't give up as you fight your way up the average gradient of over 12%. There are two sections of 1 in 4 gradient with just a brief respite where the gradient is an 'easier' 12%.

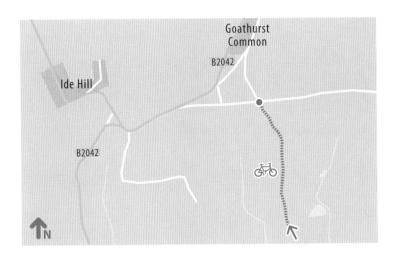

The road itself is very narrow, with mud and stones and potentially wet leaves. So despite the steepness of the ascent, it may be better to try and stay seated so you don't get rear tyre slippage. If you come to a halt here, it is nigh on impossible to get clipped back in and moving without toppling. It is a quiet back lane though, so traffic is less of a hazard.

It is (simply!) a case of fighting your way to the top now, through this dark tunnel of trees. The gradient doesn't ease now all the way to the summit, and with muscles you didn't know you had starting to burn, you continue your painful journey through the gentle S-bends.

The hurt soon ends though and as you crest the top of this wall there are just a few final metres to the T-junction, with the car park on your left. The nearest stop for a lie-down is the café at Chartwell (National Trust).

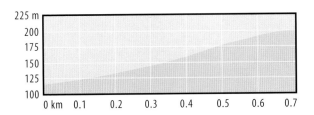

THE GRAND OLD RACE OF YORKS HILL

Catford Cycling Club have been using this challenging ascent for their hill climb com-
petition since 1935 and it has become one of the most renowned hill climbs on the
national calendar, attracting the best cycling talent and large crowds, who line the
narrow tree-covered lane. Each October, in a scene worthy of the Tour de France,
competitors surge through a tunnel of chanting spectators as they gasp their way up
the 707 yards to the top, encountering two sections of 1 in 4 gradient.

The autumnal weather often wreaks havoc on the race; in 1937 only 16 of the
92 entrants were able to get sufficient traction on the wet leaves to make it up.
Nowadays the road gets a good sweeping prior to the start, but the damp still causes
problems for many riders. Conversely the 'great storm' of 1983 wiped out many
of the trees on the climb, resulting in a tail wind that certainly assisted the winner
Phil Mason of San Fairy Ann CC, whose time of 1 minute 47.6 seconds still stands
to this day.

In 2013 four-time winner Robert Gough was finally beaten into second spot by
Matthew Pilkington, in a winning time of 1 minute 59.4 seconds. This short, steep
climb suits the powerhouse rider – often track riders have the required attributes to
do well here.

So somewhere in the region of two minutes is a very good time if you want to have
a crack at it; otherwise a trip out to watch this historic event is thoroughly recom-
mended.

(Photo: Dave Hayward)

44. TOYS HILL

Difficulty	⊘⊘⊘⊘⊘⊘⊘⊘◯◯
Distance	2.41km
Av. Gradient	6.8%
Max. Gradient	15%
Height Gain	164m
Start Point	At junction where Toys Hill Road meets South Brook Lane
Local Cafés	Chartwell (National Trust), Mapleton Road, Westerham TN16 1PS ☎ 01732 868381

The area around Bough Beech has an abundance of challenging cycling climbs, from the long, intense effort of this one to the more gradual alpine-like Ide Hill, to the wall-climbing extreme of Yorks Hill. It is great training terrain and you can really get a good workout doing loops of the area – if that happens to be your thing.

This climb is almost 2.5 kilometres long and gains an impressive 164 metres of loft. Located about 8 kilometres southwest of Sevenoaks, Toys Hill Road is just off the B2042 about a kilometre outside the village of Four Elms. We start this description where Toys Hill Road meets South Brook lane.

The first 500 metres is an opportunity to ease into this one, the legs can certainly get loose on the gentle 3% gradient though the road surface is heavy and there are quite a few potholes to mess with the rhythm.

Going under the cover of trees, things start to get harder as now the gradient

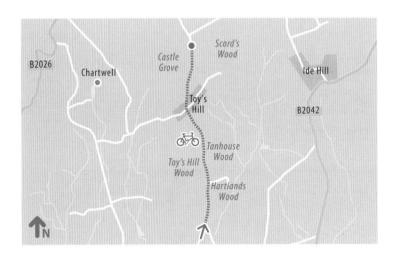

sneaks up to 7% then 8%. Riding over some shoddily repaired potholes and onto a right-hand bend the road rises again, and you may need to get out of the saddle. Passing the solitary house on the left there is a stretch of 100 metres or so of gentler pedalling before the next ramp. You now settle into a long 250-metre grind as you go by the turn to Puddledock Lane (another direction to climb up, and no easier). Try not to look up here as you may get disheartened: there is no let up just yet.

As you reach the 1.5-kilometre point it ramps up now towards 16–17%, as you crawl past Toys Hill House. Another 150 metres of toil as the gradient steadies at the 12% mark and you are willing the summit to arrive. Then finally you can drop back into the saddle as you crest onto a much easier 5% section which takes you a further 400 metres until you see the painted white lines across the road (the high point at 245 metres) and the chance to get your heart rate back down to a non-critical level.

Head to Chartwell (former family home of Winston Churchill) for a bite to eat.

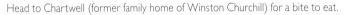

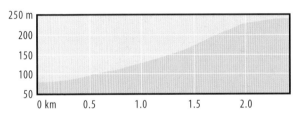

45. TITSEY HILL

Difficulty	⊙⊙⊙⊙⊙⊙⊙◑○○
Distance	1.5km
Av. Gradient	8%
Max. Gradient	16%
Height Gain	120m
Start Point	Just before Pilgrims Lane, Titsey on B269
Local Cafés	Spitfire Café, 154a Main Road, Biggin Hill, Westerham TN16 3BA ☎ 01959 571676 Botley Hill Farmhouse, Limpsfield Road, Warlingham CR6 9QH ☎ 01959 577154

Titsey Hill is well-known amongst local cyclists as an unforgiving ascent. It's particularly challenging after a hard day in the saddle, being the last climb of note as you head north towards the suburbs of South London. Some climbs have a sting in the tail; Titsey has a rude awakening right from the start, before winding through picturesque woodlands to the summit of Botley Hill, the highest point on the North Downs. The road itself, the B269, runs north from Limpsfield almost perpendicular to the popular and well-travelled Pilgrims Way.

From the tiny village of Titsey, the climb starts in earnest just after you pass the ominous 16% warning sign and the red phone box. If you've forgotten your mobile this is your last chance to call home for a lift. As the road curves to the right and you pass Pilgrims Lane and St James Church, the hill comes into view and here it really ramps up. Swiftly shifting to the largest sprocket, a 39 × 27 should get most cyclists up, but a 34 × 27 will make the first 600 metres much more bearable. Getting out of the saddle is pretty much mandatory for this section where the gradient is between 11% and 16%. The road is wide, but be aware of cars particularly on some of the sweeping bends.

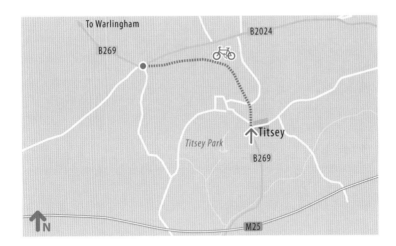

Keep plugging away past White Lane (another tough test, as climbed for the Bec CC hill climb) on your right, the road straightens through a tunnel of trees and as the lungs start to burn, the road veers to the left. With the woodland falling away dramatically on your nearside, the gradient mercifully flattens out to around 8% and some much needed respite.

You can breathe a sigh of relief, get back in the saddle and find a rhythm for the remainder of the kilometre to the top of the climb. Here, as you drop down through the gears and the gradient continues to ease, you finally you get a chance to really appreciate the scenery and the solitude of the woods. The transmitters at the top of the hill indicate that the end is in sight. Approaching the mini-roundabout, the view of the Downs opens up.

If you are in need of urgent refreshment, continue straight on for about 300 metres: tucked behind the huge barns on the left is Botley Hill Farmhouse, well known for its fantastic Sunday lunches. Alternatively, power on to the Spitfire Café in Biggin Hill, for cyclist-sized meals.

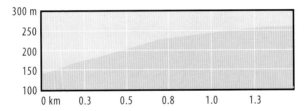

46. CARTERS HILL

Difficulty	⊙⊙⊙⊙⊙⊙⊙○○○
Distance	0.98km
Av. Gradient	10%
Max. Gradient	14%
Height Gain	98m
Start Point	At junction of Carters Hill and Underriver House Road, in village of Underriver
Local Cafés	Stefano's, 23 High Street, Seal TN15 0AN ☎ 01732 761055

This hill, 5 kilometres southeast of Sevenoaks in Kent, provides quite a challenge as you struggle with the varied gradient changes, sabotaging attempts to find any kind

of decent rhythm. Although not a long climb at just under a kilometre, it gains almost 100 metres of elevation at an average of 10%. It is a quiet back lane, so there is little traffic to be encountered, but some stones and debris often get washed into the road after a wet spell.

It starts from the small, pretty village of Underriver, at the junction of Carters Hill and Underriver House Road. Carters Hill heads in a northerly direction towards Godden Green and Seal.

Within 50 metres of the start you are struggling on a gradient of 10%; that soon rises to around 13%, as you

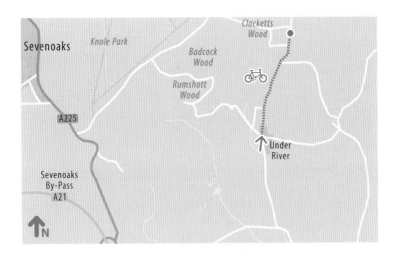

hastily click into a lower gear and push on through this first wooded section. Soon the narrow lane follows an S-bend as you come to a clearing, but you are not out of the woods just yet. Back under the cover of trees it kicks up again for a 200-metre section, touching 1 in 8 in places. With legs starting to ache, there is short-lived relief as you pass the stone-walled house on your right, the gradient easing but only for a few precious metres. It is then up a straight drag, past the vast flattened tree to the right of the road and looking ahead to the window of light at the end of this tunnel of trees.

Pretty soon you reach a left-hand bend and it kicks up again through the turn, a quick blast out of the saddle and with the summit now in sight you hit an elevation of 197 metres. There is no distinct finishing point: you hit a plateau before the road starts dropping down the other side of the hill. Continue along this road and eventually you arrive at the village of Seal and Stefano's for great pasta, panini, and the finest Italian coffee.

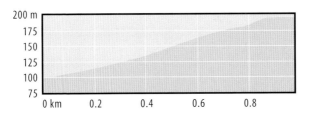

47. HOGTROUGH HILL

Difficulty	⬤⬤⬤⬤⬤⬤⬤◯◯
Distance	1.16km
Av. Gradient	8.5%
Max. Gradient	17%
Height Gain	99m
Start Point	Junction of Hogtrough Hill and Pilgrims Way
Local Cafés	Cake, 7 High Street, Downe, Orpington BR6 7US ☎ 01689 855044

Another climb in the North Downs crossing the well-travelled Pilgrims Way, Hogtrough Hill is a short, steep and challenging climb up a narrow, grass-verged lane towards Cudham/Knockholt. At just over a kilometre in length and gaining 99 metres in elevation, it averages close to 10% and will get the heart rate well and truly nearing the maximum. It is situated about 4 kilometres northeast of Westerham and if you are heading north it is an option preferable to tackling the downright unpleasant Westerham Hill. Though the road named Hogtrough Hill starts further south, we are beginning this description from the crossroads with Pilgrims Way.

First things first, you need to be extremely wary of the gravel when turning here,

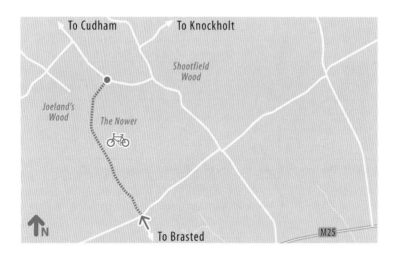

and be ready in a low gear for an immediate tough start to the ascent. Within seconds you enter gradients in excess of 12%, quickly ramping up to 18% and it's out of the saddle for the first brutal 200 metres. The lungs and legs get a real workout but it's a relatively short, sharp shock. After an S-bend a gradual easing of the gradient allows you to drop back to your saddle and you should be able to keep the gear turning whilst still seated. Here it remains at around 12% for a gentle right-hand bend, before you go under the cover of trees. The worst of this little climb is thankfully over. If you decide you want to stop, looking back down provides a fantastic view all the way back down the lane, of the vast rolling countryside and out to the crawling vehicles on the M25.

From here on the percentage stays at a much more manageable level of between 4% and 8%, so you can regain your breath, and for the next 800 metres riding through a section of woodland there is a chance to recover with a couple of small downward dips before you come to a clearing and the junction with The Nower.

Head to the village of Downe and the excellent Cake café.

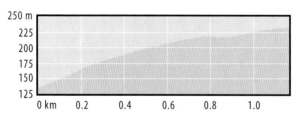

48. WHITE HILL

Difficulty	◎◎◎◎◎◎◯◯◯◯
Distance	2.59km
Av. Gradient	5.3%
Max. Gradient	12%
Height Gain	137m
Start Point	At junction of White Hill (signposted Challock) and A28, opposite Bramble Lane
Local Cafés	Crown Coffee And Gifts, 1 Church Street, Wye, Ashford TN25 5BN ☎ 01233 812798

The climb of White Hill in Kent is a lengthy 2.5 kilometres, finishing in the ancient King's Wood, former hunting ground of Henry VIII. It is located about 5 kilometres northwest of Ashford. White Hill turns off the busy A28 Canterbury Road (though if you approach from Bramble Lane opposite it would be a much more pleasant ride in), it is not a named road but follow the signs for Challock.

Setting off, you are immediately greeted with an expanse of rolling farmland ahead of you and the sight of the single-lane road disappearing into the distant woodland. There is an equally welcoming gradient for the first 200 metres and you can spin  along happily over the barely 2% incline. As the road turns left into a blind bend (keep tight to the left as the road is used as a short cut by motorists) it also begins to creep upwards on the gradient. Entering the cover of trees it nudges 7% and then 8%; be mindful of a few potholes here as you are systematically shifting down to the lower

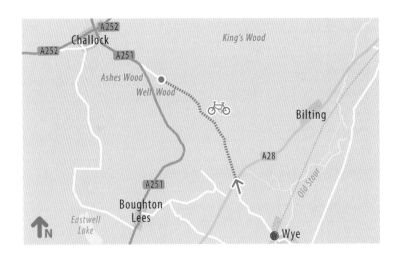

gears. Passing the bed and breakfast it stays at a fairly consistent gradient and you find yourself starting to get into some kind of a tempo. Past the noisy agricultural works on the left you then hit a section of 12%, and with a heavy road surface it feels more of a struggle; fortunately this is over fairly quickly and as you get a glimpse of the landscape on your right it eases.

Back into the denser cover of foliage the road bends to the right and there is another sapping gradient rise – you may be standing on the pedals at this point. Reaching the clearing (on your left-hand side this time), the hardest part is safely behind you and as your legs recuperate you can sneak a view of the beautiful landscape with a vista stretching for miles.

From here on in it is considerably easier riding: there is a short, flat section as you head through a narrow tunnel of trees with just a short rise of 5% to get over. But with only marginal elevation gains you come to a suitable stopping point at the King's Wood car park on the right and a total height gain of 137 metres.

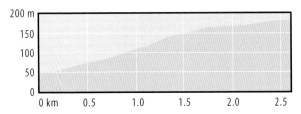

49. EXEDOWN

Difficulty	⦶ ⦶ ⦶ ⦶ ⦶ ⦶ ◯ ◯ ◯ ◯
Distance	1.47km
Av. Gradient	7.3%
Max. Gradient	16%
Height Gain	107m
Start Point	At crossroads of Kemsing Road and Exedown Road
Local Cafés	Willow Tea Rooms, 6 High Street, Otford TN14 5PQ ☎ 01959 522150

This deceptively hard climb in the North Downs of Kent is found about 3 kilometres northwest of Borough Green, and can be reached by following Pilgrims Way eastwards from Otford and onto Kemsing Road. Eventually, upon reaching a crossroads, Exedown Road (and the ascent in question) heads in a northerly direction.

The climb itself has been used several times for hill climb competitions and at almost 1.5 kilometres in length provides a stern test for cyclists of all abilities. The road surface is pretty good – but beware of vehicles swinging wide on the sharp left-hand bend midway.

From the starting point at the crossroads with Kemsing Road, the first 500 metres along Exedown Road provides nothing more than a warm-up. It is a steady 4% as you spin freely alongside rolling fields; however, you are left in no doubt as to the task ahead, with a view up to woods high above and a telecom

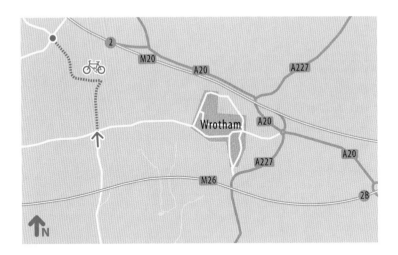

tower (which is never a good sign). As you approach a right-hand bend the road begins to steepen, before 60 metres further up you meet a very sharp left hander and the camber of the road has you out of the saddle, fighting a tricky 16% ramp. Once over this and settling back down, you can recover slightly from this burst before the ascent steepens again through an S-bend.

With the road straightening, the gradient continues to cause some suffering and getting out of the saddle eases the thighs as for the next 250 metres it doesn't let up. Riding further into the woodland scenery you curve through a right hander with the gradient still above 1 in 10, and with a final push it's around a left-hand bend and the welcome view of a flatter section. The last 200 metres stays at a gentle 4% and provides an opportunity to get your breath back and enjoy the open view over the fields to your left.

Head back along Pilgrims Way to Otford, where you can eat at the Willow Tea Rooms.

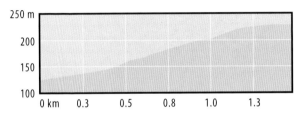

50. STAR HILL

Difficulty	⦾⦾⦾⦾⦾⦾⦾⦾○○
Distance	1.4km
Av. Gradient	7.6%
Max. Gradient	12%
Height Gain	107m
Start Point	At roundabout where A224 meets the B2211, Star Hill
Local Cafés	Cake, 7 High Street, Downe, Orpington BR6 7US ☎ 01689 855044

A regular inclusion on many cyclists' training rides, being one of the first rural climbs you can tackle upon heading out of the south London suburbs, this climb of 1.4 kilometres averages in the region of 7% and gains a total ascent of 107 metres. Probably best described as a 'slow burner', it is wise to pace yourself as often you are hanging on for the last 500 metres if you start off a bit too keenly early on!

It is located 1 kilometre northwest of the village of Dunton Green and the climb itself, up Star Hill Road, begins at the roundabout where the A224 meets the B2211

just north of the M25. It is quite apparent which direction to head in: 'Oh no, not up there' is about right. From the open fields at the start point you have a clear view of the substantial hill and the road winding upwards.

Setting off from the roundabout, the gradient gradually rises until you follow the road around to the

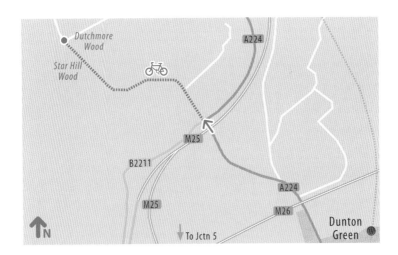

left after about 200 metres. Here the first test of 10% causes a shift down a sprocket or two. Remaining seated you can tap out a comfortable tempo for the next 250 metres at a steady 8% or so.

As you reach a long, drawn out right-hand bend it starts to smart and as you pass the white house on the right you touch a gradient of 11–12%. Now you have to grind out this next 200 metres; looking up ahead it seems the end is near but then as you go over a section of bumpy road surface and into woodland you realize the summit is still some way away.

The gradient does ease now, but if you have overdone it on the lower slopes you'll be struggling a bit. Staying at a fairly consistent 7%, you just need to keep positive over this final 250-metre stretch, through the shadows of the trees, as passing the gated entrance to Fort Halstead, a research site of the Ministry of Defence (at which Britain's development of the atomic bomb is thought to have taken place), signifies the end of this tough ascent.

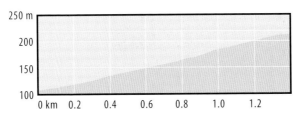

LOCAL BIKE SHOPS

Haywards Heath Cycle Centre
34–36 The Broadway, Haywards Heath,
West Sussex RH16 3AL
01444 457777
www.haywardsheathcyclecentre.com

Wealden Cycles
Unit 1 Spring Gardens, Park Lane,
Crowborough, East Sussex TN6 2QN
01892 653736
www.wealdencycles.co.uk

South Downs Bikes Ltd
28 West Street, Storrington, West Sussex
RH20 4EE
01903 745534
www.southdownsbikes.com

Cycleworks UK
19–21 West Street, Haslemere, Surrey GU27
2AB
01428 648424
www.cycleworks.co.uk/haslemere

MR Cycles
26 Clinton Place, Seaford, East Sussex, BN25
1NP
01323 893130
www.mrcycles.co.uk

Quantum Bikes
Tollgate, A27, Beddingham, Nr Lewes, East
Sussex BN8 6JZ
01273 858695
www.quantumbikes.co.uk

Pedal & Spoke
62 High Street, Cranleigh, Surrey GU6 8QG
01483 346549
www.pedalandspoke.co.uk

Pilgrim Cycles
The Old Booking Hall, Box Hill &
Westhumble Station, Westhumble Street,
Westhumble, Surrey RH5 6BT
01306 886958
www.pilgrim-cycles.co.uk

Petra Cycles
90 Station Rd East, Oxted, Surrey RH8 0QA
01883 715114
www.petracycles.co.uk

Head for the Hills
43–44 West Street, Dorking, Surrey RH4
1BU
01306 885007
www.head-for-the-hills.co.uk

Ross Cycles Ltd
145 Coulsdon Road, Caterham, Surrey CR3
5NJ
01883 331414
www.rosscycles.com

Cyclelife Petersfield
40 Dragon Street, Petersfield, Hampshire
GU31 4JJ
01730 266644
www.cyclelife.com or
www.petersfieldcycles.com

Owens Cycles
Stoner Hill, Steep, Petersfield, Hampshire
GU32 1AG
01730 260446
www.owenscycles.co.uk

Hargroves Cycles
106–108 The Hornet, Chichester, West
Sussex PO19 7JR
01243 537337
www.hargrovescycles.co.uk

Pedal On
60 Bishopswood Road, Tadley, Hampshire
RG26 4HD
01189 821021
www.pedalon.co.uk

Church Street Motorcycles (and cycles)
Church Street, Ventnor, Isle of Wight PO38 1SW
01983 852232
www.churchstreetmotorcycles.co.uk

Saddle Safari
Dean Street, Marlow, Buckinghamshire SL7 3AA
01628 477020
www.saddlesafari.co.uk

Buckingham Bikes
Villiers Buildings, Buckingham Street, Aylesbury, Buckinghamshire HP20 2LE
01296 482077
www.buckinghambikes.com

Mountain Mania Cycles
4–6 Miswell Lane, Tring, Hertfordshire HP23 4BX
01442 822458
www.mountainmaniacycles.com

Banjo Cycles
40 Bartholomew Street, Newbury, Berkshire RG14 5LL
01635 43186
www.banjocycles.com

Mitchell Cycles
7 Shrivenham Road, Swindon SN1 2QA
01793 523306
www.mitchellcycles.co.uk

Ridgeway Cycles
22 Newbury Street, Wantage, Oxfordshire OX12 8DA
01235 764445
www.ridgewaycycles.com

2 Wheels Cycles
99b High Street, Thame, Oxfordshire OX9 3EH
01844 212455
www.2wheeelsthame.co.uk

Simpson Cycles
114–116 Malden Road, Kentish Town, London NW5 4BY
020 7485 1706
www.simpsonscycles.co.uk

Future Cycles
314 Park Road, London N8 8LA
020 3538 0731
www.futurecycletraining.com

Shorter Rochford Cycles
27 Barnet Road, Potters Bar, Hertfordshire EN6 2QX
01707 662332
www.shorter-rochford.co.uk

Spokes Bikes
118 High Street, Epping CM16 4AF
01992 577702
www.spokesbikes.co.uk

Chelmer Cycles
6&7 New Writtle Street, Chelmsford, Essex CM2 0RR
01245 287600
www.chelmercycles.co.uk

The Bike Warehouse
53–55 High Street, Sevenoaks, Kent TN13 1JF
01732 464997
www.thebikewarehouse.net

Cycles UK
247 High Street, Orpington BR6 0NY
01689 898923
www.cyclesuk.com

Spiral Cycles
19 Station Road, Ashford, Kent TN23 1PP
01233 628345
www.spiralcycles.com

Larkfield Cycles
8 Martin Square, Aylesford, Kent ME20 6QJ
01732 847438
www.larkfieldcycles.co.uk

CHECKLIST

No.	Hill	Date	Time
1.	Ditchling Beacon		
2.	Cob Lane		
3.	Kidds Hill		
4.	Steyning Bostal		
5.	Tennyson's Lane		
6.	Fernden Lane		
7.	High and Over		
8.	Bo-Peep Lane		
9.	Firle Bostal		
10.	Walking Bottom		
11.	Box Hill		
12.	Chalkpit Lane		
13.	Leith Hill		
14.	Whitedown		
15.	Ranmore Common		
16.	Barhatch Lane		
17.	Succomb's Hill		
18.	Woodhill Lane		
19.	Butser Hill		
20.	Stoner Hill		
21.	Knights Hill		
22.	Watership Down		
23.	Blackgang		
24.	Wroxall Down		

No.	Hill	Date	Time
25.	Sailor's Lane		
26.	Pheasant's Hill		
27.	Dudley Lane		
28.	Kop Hill		
29.	Ivinghoe Beacon		
30.	Whitchurch Hill		
31.	Streatley Hill		
32.	Faccombe Hill		
33.	Quarry Wood		
34.	Uffington White Horse		
35.	Blowingstone Hill		
36.	Watlington Hill		
37.	Aston Hill		
38.	Swains Lane		
39.	Muswell Hill		
40.	Robins Nest Hill		
41.	Wellington Hill		
42.	North Hill		
43.	Yorks Hill		
44.	Toys Hill		
45.	Titsey Hill		
46.	Carters Hill		
47.	Hogtrough Hill		
48.	White Hill		
49.	Exedown		
50.	Star Hill